EDITIONS

ARMENIAN
BATAK/INDONESIAN
BRITISH SIGN
BULGARIAN
BURMESE (Myanmar)
CHINESE
ENGLISH
　Africa
　Australia
　Chinese/English
　India
　Indonesia
　Japan
　Korean/English
　Korean/English/
　　Japanese
　Myanmar
　Philippines
　Singapore
　Sri Lanka
　United Kingdom
　United States
ESTONIAN
FRENCH
GREEK
GUJARATI
HINDI
HUNGARIAN
IBAN/ENGLISH
ILOKANO
INDONESIAN
ITALIAN
JAPANESE
KANNADA
KISWAHILI
KOREAN
MALAYALAM
NEPALI
NORWEGIAN
ODIA
POLISH
PORTUGUESE
　Africa
　Brazil
　Portugal
RUSSIAN
SINHALA
SPANISH
　Caribbean
　Mexico
　South America
　United States
SWEDISH
TAMIL
TELUGU
THAI
URDU

THE UPPER ROOM

WHERE THE WORLD MEETS TO PRAY

Susan Hibbins
UK Editor

INTERDENOMINATIONAL
INTERNATIONAL
INTERRACIAL

36 LANGUAGES
Multiple formats are available in some languages

The Bible Reading Fellowship
15 The Chambers, Vineyard
Abingdon OX14 3FE
brf.org.uk

The Bible Reading Fellowship (BRF) is a Registered Charity (233280)

ISBN 978 0 85746 915 1
All rights reserved

Originally published in the USA by The Upper Room®
US edition © The Upper Room®
This edition © The Bible Reading Fellowship 2020
Cover image © Thinkstock

Acknowledgements

Scripture quotations marked NIV are taken from The Holy Bible, New International Version (Anglicised edition) copyright © 1979, 1984, 2011 by Biblica. Used by permission of Hodder & Stoughton Publishers, an Hachette UK company. All rights reserved. 'NIV' is a registered trademark of Biblica. UK trademark number 1448790.

Scripture quotations marked CEB are taken from the Common English Bible, CEB Copyright © 2010, 2011 by Common English Bible. Used by permission. All rights reserved worldwide. The 'CEB' and 'Common English Bible' trademarks are registered in the United States Patent and Trademark Office by Common English Bible. Use of either trademark requires the permission of Common English Bible.

Scripture quotations marked NRSV are taken from The New Revised Standard Version of the Bible, Anglicised Edition, copyright © 1989, 1995 by the Division of Christian Education of the National Council of the Churches of Christ in the USA. Used by permission. All rights reserved.

Scripture quotations marked KJV are from the Authorised Version of the Bible (The King James Bible), the rights in which are vested in the Crown, are reproduced by permission of the Crown's Patentee, Cambridge University Press.

A catalogue record for this book is available from the British Library

Printed by Gutenberg Press, Tarxien, Malta

How to use *The Upper Room*

The Upper Room is ideal in helping us spend a quiet time with God each day. Each daily entry is based on a passage of scripture, and is followed by a meditation and prayer. Each person who contributes a meditation to the magazine seeks to relate their experience of God in a way that will help those who use *The Upper Room* every day.

Here are some guidelines to help you make best use of *The Upper Room*:

1 Read the passage of scripture. It is a good idea to read it more than once, in order to have a fuller understanding of what it is about and what you can learn from it.
2 Read the meditation. How does it relate to your own experience? Can you identify with what the writer has outlined from their own experience or understanding?
3 Pray the written prayer. Think about how you can use it to relate to people you know, or situations that need your prayers today.
4 Think about the contributor who has written the meditation. Some users of the *The Upper Room* include this person in their prayers for the day.
5 Meditate on the 'Thought for the day' and the 'Prayer focus', perhaps using them again as the focus for prayer or direction for action.

Why is it important to have a daily quiet time? Many people will agree that it is the best way of keeping in touch every day with the God who sustains us, and who sends us out to do his will and show his love to the people we encounter each day. Meeting with God in this way reassures us of his presence with us, helps us to discern his will for us and makes us part of his worldwide family of Christian people through our prayers.

I hope that you will be encouraged as you use the magazine regularly as part of your daily devotions, and that God will richly bless you as you read his word and seek to learn more about him.

Susan Hibbins
UK Editor

BRF needs you!

If you're one of our thousands of regular *Upper Room* readers, you will know all about the benefits and blessings of regular Bible reading and the value of daily notes to encourage and inspire you. Readers of *The Upper Room* share those blessings with Christians across the world. In the words of UK Editor Susan Hibbins, they know that 'every day, in each part of the day, someone, somewhere is reading the same meditation'.

If you enjoy reading *The Upper Room*, and love the feeling of being part of a worldwide family, would you be willing to share your experience with others? Could you ask for a brief slot during church notices or write a short piece for your church magazine or website? Do you belong to groups, formal or informal, where you could share your experience of using Bible reading notes and encourage others to try them?

It doesn't need to be complicated or nerve-wracking: just answering these three questions in what you say or write will get your message across:

- How do Bible reading notes help you grow in your faith?
- Where, when and how do you use them?
- What would you say to people who don't already use them?

We can supply further information if you need it and would love to hear about it if you do give a talk or write an article.

For more information:

- Email **enquiries@brf.org.uk**
- Telephone BRF on **+44 (0)1865 319700** Mon–Fri 9.15–17.30
- Write to us at BRF, 15 The Chambers, Vineyard, Abingdon OX14 3FE

The most powerful witness

Utterly amazed, [those in the crowd] asked: 'Aren't all these who are speaking Galileans? Then how is it that each of us hears them in our native language?... We hear them declaring the wonders of God in our own tongues!'
Acts 2:7–8, 11 (NIV)

I grew up in a town where nearly everyone I knew was Christian. Our Christian faith was an undercurrent, a shared set of values that my friends and I rarely spoke about. When we did, I discovered that many of my friends were more insistent and vocal about their beliefs than I was. As a child, I often wondered whether my faith was lacking because I wasn't more outspoken about my belief in Christ.

As I have grown in my faith over the years – through personal practice, church membership and academic study – I have come to realise that there is no single right way to share the good news of Christ. The story of Pentecost shows us how God relates to us and how we can relate to others. It reminds us that the Holy Spirit speaks to each one of us in a way that we can understand – in a way that is familiar. Likewise, God can work through each of us in a manner well suited to our unique talents, personalities and capabilities – providing myriad opportunities for us to share our faith with others. Pentecost not only acknowledges but also celebrates the many ways we can authentically share our faith. And when we tell others about where we have seen God at work in the world, that is the most powerful witness of all.

In *The Upper Room*, people from around the globe often write about the creative ways they talk about or live their faith: from phone calls, to intercessory prayer, to giving a meal to a stranger, to asking a question in a classroom, writers share with the world their own unique experience of God's love. I hope their stories will encourage you to do the same.

Lindsay L. Gray
Editorial Director, The Upper Room

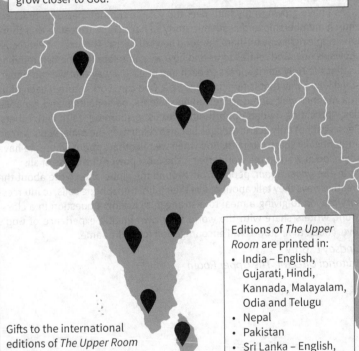

Kannada
The publishing team of *Dhyana Deepa*, the Kannada edition of *The Upper Room*, leads small-group meetings and workshops at local churches to encourage daily devotional reading as a spiritual practice and way to grow closer to God.

Malayalam
It is a goal of the Malayalam edition team to coordinate a devotional writing workshop especially for youth. They ask for prayers for their mission and ministry among young people.

Editions of *The Upper Room* are printed in:
- India – English, Gujarati, Hindi, Kannada, Malayalam, Odia and Telugu
- Nepal
- Pakistan
- Sri Lanka – English, Sinhala and Tamil

Gifts to the international editions of *The Upper Room* help the world meet to pray.
upperroom.org/gift

The Editor writes...

Recently my daily reading was Luke 5:1–11, the story of Jesus calling his first disciples. What a day that must have been. Can you imagine yourself among the crowd, listening to Jesus as he taught the people sitting in Simon's boat so that everyone could see and hear him? The sun is glittering on the water, and seagulls patrol overhead.

I wonder what Simon felt when Jesus suggested he let down the fishing nets one more time. They had been out on the water all night and had caught nothing; they were tired and dispirited. Nevertheless, because Jesus said so, Simon agreed. And what excitement followed: the nets were so full of fish that they began to break, and the boats trying to land the catch were so weighed down that they were in danger of sinking. Eager hands on shore must have pitched in to help land such a huge catch.

Amid all the excitement, noise and piles of fish, Simon suddenly falls at Jesus' feet. He is overwhelmed by Jesus' goodness contrasted with the knowledge of his own sinfulness, and so ashamed that he begs Jesus to go away from him. But Jesus reassures him: 'Don't be afraid; from now on you will fish for people' (v. 10). And Simon and his friends James and John leave their boats and everything else, and follow Jesus.

Perhaps we think, when we read about Jesus' ministry, that he might have chosen a more reliable person than Simon. Impulsive, hot-tempered, promising more than he can deliver… in fact, Simon was just like most of us: a human being who tried hard and frequently got it wrong.

It gives me comfort to know that Jesus could see beyond Simon's failings to the man he would later become. One day, Simon the fisherman would be Peter the Rock, the leader of the apostles who, after Jesus' ascension, spoke up boldly about Jesus to the crowds gathered on the day of Pentecost. Jesus' presence in all our lives helps us to be the best people we can be in his service.

Susan Hibbins
UK Editor

The Bible readings are selected with great care, and we urge you to include the suggested reading in your devotional time.

More than we asked

Read Romans 8:12–17

You didn't receive a spirit of slavery to lead you back again into fear, but you received a Spirit that shows you are adopted as [God's] children.

Romans 8:15 (CEB)

Prostate cancer had metastasised to the bones throughout my husband's body. The next morning, my first thought was: 'Earle is dying, and nothing is ever going to be all right again.' Decades of dealing with my own diagnosis of bipolar disorder had left me helpless in the world of computers, banking, investments, home and car maintenance, and looking after the garden. Earle had dealt with all of these as well as doing most of the driving. Since I had concentrated all my efforts on fighting my way out of the pit of mental illness, I had no self-confidence. I fell to my knees and asked for the help that only God can give.

God gave me strength as I started to learn all the responsibilities that I might soon have to deal with on my own – banking, making appointments, driving Earle and myself, moving into a smaller home. Then, after God was faithful in getting rid of my fears and giving me the ability to cope, Earle began to respond well to the cancer treatment. Though not in remission, Earle's cancer is controlled.

Now able to do many things that had seemed beyond my capabilities before, I am sharing with Earle the abundant life that Jesus promised to us if we would trust in him.

Prayer: *Faithful God, we rejoice in your goodness. Thank you for physical healing and for the spiritual healing only you can provide. Amen*

Thought for the day: Jesus offers me abundant life.

Darlene Forgues (Alberta, Canada)

Never too late

Read Luke 15:11–32

You were washed, you were sanctified, you were justified in the name of the Lord Jesus Christ and by the Spirit of our God.
1 Corinthians 6:11 (NIV)

As part of my responsibilities as a chaplain at a local hospital, I was called to the bedside of an elderly woman. I found her shouting out in anguish to Jesus and then to me. She had been diagnosed with a brain haemorrhage and was afraid she would die and not go to heaven. When I asked the reason for her fear, she explained that her sins were just too great.

I reminded her of the parable of the prodigal son and how our Father in heaven will welcome us back with open arms. She told me she was afraid it was too late. I assured her that if Jesus could forgive the thief on the cross next to him, the same is true for all of us. We then prayed together, and a great peace seemed to come over her. When I saw her again the next morning, she took my hand and said that she knew she was forgiven and welcomed back by God.

No matter what sins we may have committed, whether we are coming to Christ for the first time or returning to God like the prodigal son, we don't have to be afraid that our sins are too great. Instead, we can reach out to our Father and remember that God forgives and welcomes us with open arms.

Prayer: *Dear Father, remind us that it is never too late to turn to you. Help us to be open to receive your love and forgiveness. Amen*

Thought for the day: It is never too late to seek God's forgiveness.

Scott Martin (New Jersey, US)

PRAYER FOCUS: THOSE WHO FEEL UNWORTHY

Resting on a rock

Read Mark 1:35–39

Jesus often withdrew to lonely places and prayed.
Luke 5:16 (NIV)

Once or twice a year, my husband's uncle drove from his Indiana home to a north-western desert. He said he needed to get away from every-thing and spend some time just sitting on a rock. He usually combined his trips with mission work, meeting various needs in the area. First, however, he withdrew to his rock to clear his mind and calm his spirit from the stresses of life.

Whether he intentionally followed Jesus' example or simply recog-nised his personal need for solitude, he never said. Either way, his actions demonstrated the pattern that Jesus set during his time on earth. Jesus' life was certainly full. He ministered to hurting crowds through healing, feeding and teaching. He offered unconditional love. He touched lepers. He ate with outcasts. He challenged the status quo. But even with all that interaction, Jesus regularly withdrew from everyone and everything for time alone with his Father.

Don't we need the same renewal? If we go at life non-stop, we deplete all our energy and become no good to ourselves or anyone else. Personal time with God, who is our rock, restores our energy and prepares us for another day of loving obedience to our Father.

Prayer: *Thank you, Father, for meeting us in solitude and giving us strength when we turn to you. Amen*

Thought for the day: Where do I spend one-on-one time with God?

Diana C. Derringer (Kentucky, US)

Small acts

Read Matthew 25:31–40

The King will reply, 'Truly I tell you, whatever you did for one of the least of these brothers and sisters of mine, you did for me.'
Matthew 25:40 (NIV)

As I left the cafe carrying my takeaway, I saw a person sitting on the pavement nearby. As I approached, I leaned over and asked, 'Would you like something to eat?' He responded with 'Yes!' As I shared my food with him, four or five people walking behind me leaned over and put money in his hat. As I got into my car, I began thinking about how giving to others leaves me feeling joyful.

I then thought about all the easy ways that I can give to others every day. I can buy extra food at the supermarket and make extra portions of dinner to give to people in need. I can carry bottles of water in my car to hand out to people who are homeless. I can stop and talk with people I meet, sharing time with them. Even while driving, I can be courteous to other drivers. When I'm waiting in a queue I can allow someone who looks rushed and harried to go ahead of me. Through these and other small acts of mercy we can share God's love with the world and fill our own hearts with joy.

Prayer: *Dear God, every day show us those who need what we can give as we pray, 'Father, hallowed be your name, your kingdom come. Give us each day our daily bread. Forgive us our sins, for we also forgive everyone who sins against us. And lead us not into temptation.'* Amen*

Thought for the day: 'It is more blessed to give than to receive' (Acts 20:35).

Dean T. Skoglund (Minnesota, US)

Peace and comfort

Read Philippians 4:6–9

The prayer of a righteous person is powerful and effective.
James 5:16 (NIV)

One evening, as I was preparing supper for the family, a saucepan full of milk boiled over and poured from the stove on to my right leg – from my knee down to my foot. I cried out and managed to put my pain-wracked leg under running water. When I remembered that I was scheduled to speak the very next day at church in my village and then three days later at a church in another town, negative and fearful thoughts and questions began to surface: 'How will I walk to speak at church tomorrow? Should I send a message to the town church and tell them I cannot come?' These thoughts were joined by mental images of being in the hospital with a suspended leg. I was even thinking I might be scarred for life.

Then suddenly I realised that I was not listening to the Lord. So I switched to reading Bible verses that talk about healing, and I started to pray. At this point, I could feel the pain even deep inside the leg, and it was excruciating. Yet, by the time I had finished praying, all the pain was gone and no scar was left on my leg.

When we face difficult situations, worry and fear quickly grip us. But they do not solve any problems. What peace and comfort prayer and faith in God provide!

Prayer: *Dear Lord, when we get into trouble, help us to look to you in faith and prayer instead of worrying. In Jesus' name. Amen*

Thought for the day: Praying solves more problems than worrying does.

Charity M. Kiregyera (Kampala, Uganda)

PRAYER FOCUS: SOMEONE INJURED IN AN ACCIDENT AT HOME

A Lenten challenge

Read Philemon 4–7

Do not withhold good from those to whom it is due, when it is in your power to act.
Proverbs 3:27 (NIV)

During Lent our minister challenged us to step out of our comfort zone by faithfully tithing, sharing the gospel with others and helping our community through acts of service. I accepted the challenge. My first payday during Lent brought the biggest pay cheque I had ever received. Although it was just a few mouse clicks on my computer, sending ten per cent of that pay cheque to the church was tough. Next, I posted on social media about my faith and included an open invitation for questions and for anyone to join me at church. The positive outpouring of Christian love was amazing.

Finally, I discovered that a group from church served a meal at a homeless shelter once a month. Now I look forward to the fourth Saturday of every month and make every effort to participate.

I used to think that money was too tight and that I was too busy for any of these ministries. Now I know that, through faith, we are all capable of doing what God's word calls us to do. I remain busy with family and work obligations, but I try my best to look for opportunities to show God's love through works of faith.

Prayer: *Heavenly Father, we give you thanks for all you have done for us and all you allow us to do in your name. Keep showing us the joys of serving you. In Jesus' name. Amen*

Thought for the day: I can follow God's word no matter how committed I am.

Bryan Young (Texas, US)

Quest for the queen

Read 2 Corinthians 5:6–9

Heaven is declaring God's glory; the sky is proclaiming his handiwork.
Psalm 19:1 (CEB)

A queen bee nestled in her hive can be quite elusive. I'm pretty good at finding hidden objects in a picture game on a page, but as a new beekeeper, I worried about finding our queen. My husband Joe and I spent several months studying the care of bees before purchasing a hive from a local beekeeper. Our 'starter pack' of bees, derived from a larger colony, came with five frames containing comb and larvae to put in our hive, along with the worker bees and a queen. 'What if we don't see the queen?' I asked Joe as we left with our boxed bees.

'Don't worry,' he said. 'You don't have to see the queen. If you see her eggs and developing larvae, you know she's there.' About a week later, curiosity moved me to look in our hive. I saw newly laid eggs and growing larvae in different stages of development. Joe was right. I never saw the queen, but I saw her handiwork.

Our search for God can be much like my quest for the queen bee. We long to see God but because he is invisible, we get discouraged. Yet, if we take time to look, we see signs of God's presence around us. Just as I haven't seen my queen bee, I haven't seen God face-to-face – but I have seen his handiwork.

Prayer: *Dear Lord, give us eyes to see you and faith to believe. Amen*

Thought for the day: Every day I can see God revealed in all creation.

Suzanne Montgomery (Indiana, US)

Chosen

Read 1 Peter 2:1–10

You are a chosen people, a royal priesthood, a holy nation, God's special possession, that you may declare the praises of him who called you out of darkness into his wonderful light.
1 Peter 2:9 (NIV)

I hurried to the sports centre near my house, excited to try out for the local five-a-side football team. After doing exercises and using our skills for a while, we gathered to hear who had been chosen to be part of the team. I was hopeful, but unfortunately I was not chosen. Dejected, I slowly walked home.

Most people can probably identify with this experience – whether it was not being selected to be part of a team, not being accepted into the college of their choice or not being chosen for their dream job. When we aren't included or chosen, we can become discouraged. But even when others find us unsuitable, we have been chosen to be members of God's family. What a privilege! Furthermore, we have been chosen to 'declare the praises' of God, who called us out of darkness into his light. We are his ambassadors, proclaiming the message of reconciliation to the world.

When we feel insignificant and unwanted, we can remember our family and our high calling. We are God's children, and we are his royal ambassadors.

Prayer: *Dear God, thank you for choosing us. Help us to remember that we have an honourable calling. Amen*

Thought for the day: God will always choose me.

Wayne Greenawalt (Illinois, US)

Grateful expectation

Read Colossians 1:1–14

*We continually ask God to fill you with the knowledge of his will...
being strengthened with all power according to his glorious might so
that you may have great endurance and patience.*
Colossians 1:9, 11 (NIV)

For a few years, I have had to wait for God to heal my son. Some days
my faith has been strong, and I have felt positive and hopeful. At other
times, I have let fear creep in and cause me to doubt and then have
slipped into deep sorrow. I continued with this cycle of highs and lows
until I found the verses above from Colossians.

In this passage, Paul prayed that the believers in Colossae would
be strengthened with patience and joyful longsuffering. The word
'patience' refers to being able to accept or tolerate delay without getting angry or upset. It can also mean cheerful or hopeful endurance.
Paul was acknowledging that at times heaven will be silent and we will
have to wait.

As difficult as it may sound, God wants us to wait with an attitude
of joy. These scripture verses suggest to me that while we wait for an
erring child to return home, we can rejoice. While we pray for our life
partner to appear, we can rejoice. While we wait for a baby to be con-
ceived, we can rejoice and give thanks to God, who has already given us
far greater blessings than what we desire for the future. And while we
wait, God is close beside us.

Prayer: *Dear Father, strengthen us so that we can wait patiently with a
sense of grateful expectation. Amen*

Thought for the day: I will choose to praise God in all situations.

Lilian Nwanze Akobo (Meath, Ireland)

A room fully prepared

Read John 14:1–4

My Father's house has many rooms; if that were not so, would I have told you that I am going there to prepare a place for you?
John 14:2 (NIV)

Three days before my birthday I was feeling the full effects of my chemotherapy treatment. My mother telephoned, full of excitement that my husband and I were coming home to celebrate my birthday. I told her how awful I felt, but she told me she would prepare my room for me and give me the best medicine in the world – a mother's love. Two days later my brother called to tell me that Mother had died in her sleep. When I arrived at my parents' house, I found my room fully prepared just as my mother had promised. In the kitchen the ingredients were set out to make my favourite meal. My mother's last acts on earth were finding ways to comfort me as I endured my battle with cancer.

In today's reading, as Jesus was about to face a horrible death, he reassured his followers that he would prepare a room for them. Our parents' love for us can be a reminder of the loving sacrifice Jesus made for us. I know that Jesus has a room prepared for me, and I know that my mother is there waiting for me. As I celebrate Mothering Sunday this year, I will worship my Saviour and remember my mother and her great love for me; and I will remember that Jesus has prepared a room for us all.

Prayer: *O God, thank you for human families and the love we can share. Most of all, thank you for your Son, Jesus Christ, who taught us how to love. Amen*

Thought for the day: God's love for me never dies.

Karan Young (Texas, US)

Iron sharpens iron

Read 2 Timothy 2:14–19

*Do your best to present yourself to God as one approved by him,
a worker who has no need to be ashamed, rightly explaining the
word of truth.*
2 Timothy 2:15 (NRSV)

During the past school year, a colleague and friend approached me and
suggested I start a Bible study for teachers. After some thought and
prayer, I decided to send an email to teachers and other staff inviting
them to my classroom for Bible study before school began on Tuesdays
and Fridays. I had no idea what to expect. But on Tuesdays we studied
the book of James and on Fridays the book of Philippians.

In Proverbs, we are told that 'as iron sharpens iron, so one person
sharpens another' (27:17, NIV). It took several meetings for trust to
build, but we discovered that as we studied together we grew as friends.
We became more willing to share our struggles with one another. We
listened to one another. We prayed with one another. We encouraged
one another – even checking on those who missed a meeting. God truly
worked in our midst, encouraging us through scripture and through
fellowship. Most of all, God helped each of us learn to rely more upon
the working of the Holy Spirit in all our relationships with one another,
with our students and with him.

Prayer: *Dear Father, thank you for the Bible. Help us to grow as we read
it, and lead us to find others who will faithfully study with us. Amen*

Thought for the day: Bible study helps me grow in my relationship
with God and with others.

Michael W. Martin (North Carolina, US)

God provides

Read 2 Corinthians 9:10–15

Cast all your anxiety on [God] because he cares for you.
1 Peter 5:7 (NIV)

Following the birth of my first child, I had postnatal depression, and my husband was facing unemployment. It became clear that a career change was on the horizon for him, which added to the uncertainty we felt about the future. My husband and I both felt anxious about what was next for our family; we even thought we might need to move to another area of the country.

One morning my son was crying to be fed. As I prepared a bottle for him, I said, 'Calm down, sweetheart. When have I ever not given you what you need?' As I said this, I realised that I had been crying out to Jesus in fear about how and when my family's needs would be met. I saw myself as a scared child, in need of something that I could not provide for myself. As I looked at my son, I knew that in a short while the sustenance he was waiting for would be provided – he would be full, content and happy.

What a picture of how Christ cares for us! In all my worry, Christ was near, inviting me to cast my fear, anxiety, doubt and anger on him. Like a loving parent, God can and will provide for our needs.

Prayer: *Loving God, when we can't see the way forward, help us to trust that you can. Amen*

Thought for the day: God will provide for me.

Courtney Boulware (Ohio, US)

ust through prayer

Read Mark 11:19–24

Therefore I tell you, whatever you ask for in prayer, believe that you have received it, and it will be yours.
Mark 11:24 (NIV)

As my wife and I finished dinner one evening, we got a phone call from my sister-in-law. She told us that her husband had been in an accident and had suffered a serious head injury. Shocked, my wife and I immediately left to meet her relatives at the hospital. The doctor told me that my brother-in-law had only a one per cent chance of survival. He soon underwent an operation, fell into a coma and was put on a ventilator. The doctors gave us no hope that he would survive due to the large amount of blood he had lost.

Prayer has immense power. Because I have witnessed the way that prayer can save lives, my wife and I started praying, despite our fears. Two days later, my brother-in-law came out of his coma. The doctors and our family were amazed that he had survived. My faith in God is now stronger because I witnessed the power of prayer. When we trust God, our faith can grow stronger than our fears.

Prayer: *Dear God, help us to feel your presence during difficult times. Amen*

Thought for the day: I express my trust in God when I pray.

Rajeev Ranjan Pandey (Uttar Pradesh, India)

Always ready

Read 1 Peter 3:13–17

Always be prepared to give an answer to everyone who asks you to give the reason for the hope that you have.
1 Peter 3:15 (NIV)

As a bird lover, I was delighted to see that the lakeside where my husband and I had built our house was a great habitat for a variety of birds. Anticipating opportunities to photograph them, I bought a better camera. When I was experimenting with it, a pair of snow geese paid a visit and I was able to take photos of those beautiful birds. It was a good thing, because they were gone the next day.

Birds don't willingly pose, so if I want photos of them, I have to be prepared – to have my camera with me and wait for my chance. Even then, I may not be successful in getting a good photograph. But the opportunities will continue to come; if I don't leave my camera on the shelf, I won't regret the great photographs that could have been.

We don't always know when a chance to witness to the hope we have in Christ will come. But by being open to the urging of the Holy Spirit and willing to share our story, we are ready to do so. And who knows? Maybe someone will cross our path who needs to experience the hope found only in our Saviour. How ready will we be to share God's story?

Prayer: *O Lord, may the hope you give us be so evident that others will want to hear about it. Help us to be ready for opportunities to witness to your love and salvation. Amen*

Thought for the day: How will I express my hope in Christ today?

Lori Herold (Illinois, US)

Moving with God

Read Psalm 143:5–10

Teach me to do what pleases you, because you are my God. Guide me by your good spirit into good land.
Psalm 143:10 (CEB)

Even though my husband and I have moved house 21 times, I still find change difficult – it tends to bring out all my insecurities and worries. One move was especially hard for me. I loved the place where we lived; we were part of a great church and would be leaving many friends. I worked at a large walk-in centre helping women in crisis, and felt that my job was also my ministry.

Only later did I realise God's purpose for the move. It enabled me to work in a similar organisation that was struggling – and God used my experience to help them grow. I began to look back on other moves and could see that God was at work every time. Through all my family's changes, I have learned that I can trust God to lead me in the right direction.

When faced with an opportunity that requires change, we can ask God to guide and direct us. Because God loves us and wants us to lead lives of significance and meaningful service, he will answer our prayers for direction – not only through scripture but also through the wisdom of Christian friends and mentors. God's answer may not always be what we prefer to do, but we can know that following his direction is always best.

Prayer: *Dear God, help us to trust that you will show us the ways and places where we can continue to find joy in serving you. Amen*

Thought for the day: I can trust God to show me the best way to serve.

Myrna Conrad (Florida, US)

When life hurts

Read Matthew 5:1–12

Blessed are those who mourn, for they will be comforted.
Matthew 5:4 (NRSV)

In July 2012, my wife Joyce died suddenly within 48 hours after taking me back home after emergency surgery to save my leg. I was bereft. Not only was Joyce my best friend, my wife of 35 years and the mother of our two children; she was also my partner in ministry and a multi-talented musician and university teacher with a radiant personality.

Two blessings were critical for me in her loss. First, a conviction that Jesus knew what he was talking about when he said, 'Blessed are those who mourn, for they will be comforted.' There were many days – especially in the first two years – when I would weep and scream in the pain of that loss. The scream was not 'Why?' just 'It hurts.'

The second blessing came the day after Joyce's death as I heard the Holy Spirit ask me this question: 'If you could swap your years with Joyce and not have this pain, would you do it?' My immediate answer was, 'Absolutely not.'

Now the pain has dulled and is far less frequent. Every day I have continued to give thanks for Joyce – the life and love we shared and the family God entrusted to us.

Prayer: *Thank you, Jesus, for your presence and guidance through scripture and the Holy Spirit. Amen*

Thought for the day: Even in my grief, God blesses me.

Torrey Curtis (Oklahoma, US)

Hills of life

Read 2 Corinthians 4:7–18

This slight momentary affliction is preparing us for an eternal weight of glory beyond all measure.
2 Corinthians 4:17 (NRSV)

When I was at high school, we had 'hills day'. A group of us jogged to a hill that overlooks a lake, and the teacher called out, 'Ten times, up and down.' The first two laps were invigorating because the group tackled the hill together. But by lap nine, I was alone, my sides ached and I gasped for breath; I wanted to give up. Though only creeping forward, I forced one foot in front of the other, determined to finish. When I reached the top of the hill for the tenth time, I looked out across the expanse of the lake. It stretched so far that it made me – and the hill – seem small.

Years later I saw how much that hill was similar to life. Sometimes life is fun, like the jog from the school to the hill. At other times putting one foot in front of the other is gruelling. However, when we face the hills of life, we can focus on Christ, who climbed a hill and carried a cross for us, giving us the hope of eternity. As we do, our trials look smaller.

Prayer: *Dear Father, help us to lift our eyes to you in challenging times. Remind us that our earthly troubles will seem small when we stand in the presence of your glory. Amen*

Thought for the day: How does my outlook change when I focus on Christ?

C. Jennings (Ontario, Canada)

The ultimate connection

Read John 15:1–10

My Father is glorified by this, that you bear much fruit and become my disciples.

John 15:8 (NRSV)

On the island of Trinidad, where I grew up, some of the agricultural crops are pumpkin, watermelon, passion fruit and tomatoes. All these fruits grow on vines.

In John 15, Jesus spoke about a vineyard. The purpose of the vine is to provide support and to send food and water to the branches. As long as the branches are connected to the vine, they will bear fruit. Occasionally the gardener must prune the branches. This process is important because it maintains the health of the branches, strengthens them and encourages them to produce more fruit.

Jesus is our vine and we are his branches. As long as we are connected to Jesus, we will be provided with the nourishment, support and love that we need to live as true followers of Christ. Staying connected to Jesus involves studying the Bible, prayer and fellowship with other believers. The Holy Spirit works within us to bear fruit. Our fruit consists of godly actions, such as forgiveness and compassion. Our obedience to Jesus' commands brings glory to God.

Prayer: *Thank you, Jesus, for giving us your strength and support. Help us to remain connected to you so that we may bear much good fruit. Amen*

Thought for the day: How do I stay connected to Jesus?

Renae Aberdeen (Indiana, US)

The power of presence

Read Luke 10:38–42

Mary has chosen the better part, which will not be taken away from her.

Luke 10:42 (NRSV)

I remember having long talks with my girlfriend Melissa discussing the day's activities, our plans, our goals, our future married life. Then there were the long pauses, maybe lasting as much as ten minutes, when neither of us spoke. Yet we were connected, and somehow that was important. On long drives, walks in the park or just sitting in the house, that same silence continues to be part of our relationship. Sometimes just being present with one another is enough. I realise that truth even more fully when we are absent from each other. Presence matters.

In today's reading, we see that Mary understood the value of presence. She didn't have to join in the conversation. She didn't have to be the centre of attention. Just to be present at Jesus' feet was enough. For her presence, Jesus rewarded her: 'Mary has chosen the better part, which will not be taken away from her.' What praise from the Master for simply being present with him!

God still seeks our presence. In the hustle and bustle of each busy day, let us find time to sit quietly with Christ. In those precious moments of solitude may we discover intimacy beyond words, for when we draw near to God, he will draw near to us (see James 4:8).

Prayer: *O God, teach us to recognise your presence, and help us to stay connected with you throughout this day. Amen*

Thought for the day: I will set aside time for Christ today.

Kevin Thomas (Alabama, US)

On assignment

Read John 5:19–24

I can do nothing on my own. As I hear, I judge; and my judgement is just, because I seek to do not my own will but the will of him who sent me.

John 5:30 (NRSV)

When I received several requests to participate in ministries and projects that I felt were not in keeping with what God had called me to do, my friend Ann suggested that I write a mission statement. I thought mission statements were only for companies and businesses, but with Ann's encouragement I wrote three points that I felt were key to God's calling for me. Now when people urge me to get involved with their projects, I am able to use my mission statement to help me decide whether they fit in with God's plans for me.

Similarly, Jesus had a mission. Jesus said, 'I can do nothing on my own… I seek to do not my own will but the will of him who sent me.' Although few people understood Jesus' mission, he remained focused on the work God gave him.

Like Jesus, we all have work to do. If we don't know what that is, we can ask, and God will guide us. When we know our assignment, we can remain focused on our mission.

Prayer: *Dear Lord, thank you for entrusting us with your work while we are here on earth. In the name of Jesus. Amen*

Thought for the day: What is my mission statement?

Mary E. Webb (New Mexico, US)

Everyone's gift matters

Read 1 Corinthians 12:14–26

If one member suffers, all suffer together with it; if one member is honoured, all rejoice together with it.
1 Corinthians 12:26 (NRSV)

After having surgery on one of my big toes, I needed crutches for support and weeks of recovery. My entire daily life seemed to revolve around that toe and its healing. I had never said to a friend, 'Let me show you my wonderful toe! It helps me so much every day!' But after this experience I felt a new appreciation for its importance.

The way I undervalued my toe made me think about the parts of the body of Christ – the church. Some people have roles to play that often go unnoticed, yet they serve important functions in God's work. I think of the editors who make a writer's work clearer, the people who quietly pray for others and the cleaning team who keep church facilities tidy and ready for study and worship each week. The list goes on. How often do we take the time to acknowledge and encourage others? Paul reminds us that when any member suffers, we all suffer; and when any member is honoured, we rejoice together. When members of our Christian family are hurting in some way, we can support and encourage one another, renewing our strength for the tasks God has assigned us. When we care for and value one another, it is cause for rejoicing.

Prayer: *Dear God, help us to see the value of other Christians and to commend them for their work. Amen*

Thought for the day: Today I will show my gratitude for the contributions of others to God's work.

Linda Neff (Ontario, Canada)

Bold encouragement

Read Ecclesiastes 4:9–12

Encourage one another and build each other up.
1 Thessalonians 5:11 (NIV)

The swimming competition we were attending was crowded with children, including our two grandsons. Slade, the older of the two, had finished competing in his age group and was now at the side of the pool, rooting for his younger brother, Grant. Even over the noise of the crowd, we heard Slade calling, 'Come on, Grant, keep going. You can make it!' As I watched him, I thought, 'He doesn't care at all about what the crowd thinks of him and his jumping up and down and yelling. He's more concerned that his brother finishes the race.'

When later I thought about the unashamed way my grandson had encouraged his brother, I asked myself, 'Am I as zealous as Slade in my encouragement for my brothers and sisters in Christ?' I'm ashamed that the answer is no. Unlike my young grandson, I am often inhibited by my fear of what others will think. Slade inspired me to ask God for forgiveness and also for boldness to encourage others.

Prayer: *Dear Lord Jesus, help us to reflect your nature in our actions towards others each day. We pray as you taught us, 'Our Father which art in heaven, Hallowed be thy name. Thy kingdom come. Thy will be done, as in heaven, so in earth. Give us day by day our daily bread. And forgive us our sins; for we also forgive every one that is indebted to us. And lead us not into temptation; but deliver us from evil.'* Amen*

Thought for the day: To whom will I speak an encouraging word in Christ's name today?

George Childree (Alabama, US)

*Luke 11:2–4 (KJV)

Fear-conquering love

Read Matthew 6:25–34

*Do not worry about tomorrow, for tomorrow will worry about itself.
Each day has enough trouble of its own.*
Matthew 6:34 (NIV)

Once again, I felt paralysed and completely helpless. As the darkness of my bedroom closed in on me, panic rose in my chest. All too often, fear seemed to rule my life. Questions about my future, my career, my financial situation, my rocky relationship with my significant other, my ill family members – the list was endless – gnawed at my mind.

As I lay on my back staring at the ceiling, I remembered the words of Matthew 6:34 quoted above. I realised how much this never-ending cycle of fear, with its tossing and turning at night and worrying by day, was hurting my spiritual life, as it controlled my thoughts and actions. However, I knew that Jesus loves me and died to save me and that he is sovereign over all.

As the apostle John wrote, fear cannot exist where love is in complete control; if I fear, I am not made perfect in love (see 1 John 4:18). I mentally recited all the ways in which God had provided for me time and time again. As I reflected, I realised that through every trial, Jesus was present and had never failed to give me what I needed. Taking a deep breath, I prayed, telling God about all my worries and fears and praying for peace before I drifted off to sleep.

Prayer: *Dear God, give us a deeper understanding of your love so that fear no longer rules our lives. Amen*

Thought for the day: Because of God's love for me, fear and worry do not have to rule my life.

Laura Rothhaar (Ohio, US)

PRAYER FOCUS: THOSE WHO STRUGGLE WITH INSOMNIA

I belong!

Read 1 John 3:1–2

Now if we are children, then we are heirs – heirs of God and co-heirs with Christ, if indeed we share in his sufferings in order that we may also share in his glory.
Romans 8:17 (NIV)

Nearly everyone wants to feel they belong – that they are part of a group, have a cultural identity and are accepted. Though this need is often associated with our teenage years, we all have it. Despite having the same surname, some people do not experience the joy of belonging to a family, of being part of a joint history. Many people have no one with whom to share their joy and hope or their sorrow and fear.

In my ministry, I meet many people who come to church alone and become part of a new family – the family of God. In Christ, we became co-heirs of the kingdom of God. The family of faith can create space for new beginnings, renewed hopes for living this life and new hope in life eternal. It is God's wish that we become part of his family. Jesus taught this when he instructed the disciples to begin their prayer by saying, 'Our Father'. Jesus shared the glory of the Father with his disciples and with all of us. Everyone is welcome in the family of faith because our heavenly Father loves us.

Prayer: *Lord Jesus, thank you for making us a part of your family of faith. Help us to invite others to find in you a real sense of being a family. In your name, we pray. Amen*

Thought for the day: I belong to Christ's family of faith.

Marcos Antonio Garcia (São Paulo, Brazil)

Running away

Read Psalm 139:1–12

The Lord will keep you from all harm – he will watch over your life.
Psalm 121:7 (NIV)

When I was young, I often ran away from home. I thought you had to actually run to run away, so off I would go down the road. I wouldn't get far before my brother would catch up and bring me home. I always knew he would come and get me.

My brother joined the army in 1946, on his 17th birthday. He had been my confidant, adviser and protector, and I missed him terribly. While away, he wrote me letters filled with wise advice and promises that he would come home and keep me safe. I still have those letters. He came home for a visit after several months, and when it was time for him to leave again, I cried and begged him to stay. I even refused to go to the railway station to see him off. I didn't know that the next time I'd see him would be three months later, when his coffin would arrive at that same station. He died of pneumonia as a complication of kidney disease.

I never physically ran away after that, but I ran in other ways. This time, God came after me. He brought me to a church where people took me in and showed me the love of Christ. I am eternally grateful for the church that set me on the path which changed my life. Although I have strayed from that path since, God has always brought me back.

Prayer: *Redeeming God, thank you for bringing us back when we run away. Thank you for the people you have placed in our lives who love us, watch over us and protect us. Amen*

Thought for the day: How can I help bring others back to God?

Grace Epperson (Michigan, US)

Content where I am

Read 2 Samuel 7:18–29

Then King David went in and sat before the Lord, and he said: 'Who am I, Sovereign Lord, and what is my family, that you have brought me this far?'

2 Samuel 7:18 (NIV)

I'm thankful for the lovely part of the world I live in. Lakes, rivers, mountains and the sea are all just a short drive away. I often go out and photograph wildlife like sea lions, eagles and white-tailed deer.

But one morning, I struggled with envy of others who've travelled to exotic places that I haven't been to. Instead of dwelling on these thoughts, though, I decided to spend extra time reading my Bible, because I knew God would encourage me to be content with my corner of the world. I brushed aside my craving for places I have not been to, and I opened the word of God instead.

As I was reading David's prayer about being humbled that his family would be remembered by the Lord forever, I realised my foolishness in coveting anything earthly. Just like David, all those who trust in the Lord will be established for eternity in God's kingdom. I was reminded of how much more important heaven is compared to earthly things. Heaven's shores will forever be more breathtaking than all the exotic places the world has to offer.

Prayer: *Dear God, thank you for the beauty of the world in which we live. Help us to remember that heaven's joys will far surpass earthly ones. Amen*

Thought for the day: When I'm feeling discontented, I can turn to scripture for encouragement.

Wendy L. Macdonald (British Columbia, Canada)

A change of heart

Read 1 Corinthians 9:20–23

There is neither Jew nor Gentile, neither slave nor free, nor is there male and female, for you are all one in Christ Jesus.
Galatians 3:28 (NIV)

At our farewell luncheon at the church where I had been minister for five years, the group was surprised when George spoke. He was a retired businessman who had always sat quietly with his wife at the very back of the church. That day, in a shaky voice, George said something that touched every heart there: 'Pastor Koo, in five years you have made us cry twice. The first time was five years ago, when we received news that we were to have a Korean pastor. The second time is today, the day that you and your family leave us. The first were tears over having our first cross-cultural/cross-racial pastor; now they are tears of love and sadness as we see you and your family go.' Not long after we left, George passed away.

His words became a great motivation and encouragement for me in my ministry. As is written in today's quoted verse from Galatians – despite our prejudice, differences and anxiety, we are all one in Christ Jesus. Still today, George reminds me that God's ministry is not fulfilled by words but when we meet heart to heart in Christ's love.

Prayer: *Dear Father, remind us that through your power we can overcome all worldly hurdles to minister to others. Amen*

Thought for the day: Every day, God strengthens me for ministry to others.

KyungMo Koo (Maryland, US)

God's love endures

Read Romans 5:1–11

Suffering produces endurance, and endurance produces character, and character produces hope, and hope does not disappoint us.
Romans 5:3–5 (NRSV)

It started with a twinge of pain in my leg, but the little twinges soon became greater and steadily intensified. Two years later, while I was sitting in my high school maths class, I was told to go to the head teacher's office. I could feel my heart pounding as I walked along the corridor and felt it sink when I saw my parents sitting with the head teacher. They told me that my doctor had diagnosed me with chronic osteomyelitis and said they needed to take me to hospital for an emergency biopsy. I was filled with fear. I didn't understand why this was happening to me or why God had allowed so much pain to enter my life. However, five years later, I know that without this experience I would not have become the person I am today.

Although the pain still takes over at times, I look to God to fill my spirit with hope and endurance. I know there is suffering in the world that far surpasses anything I will ever experience, and I continue to pray for those who are afflicted. Jesus suffered on the cross, and he understands our pain. Regardless of our earthly suffering, we can trust that God's love will outlast it all.

Prayer: *Dear God, guide us when we face illness and pain. Give us a renewed sense of hope and faith in your love. Amen*

Thought for the day: God fills me with hope and helps me endure.

Candyce Sturgeon (North Carolina, US)

Distracting pride

Read Philippians 4:10–19

My God will meet all your needs according to the riches of his glory in Christ Jesus.

Philippians 4:19 (NIV)

During my first hiking trip, I wasn't far into the trek up the mountain when I realised that I had seriously overpacked. As I struggled, I saw a member from our group, whom I had yet to meet, coming back down the path towards me. 'Please, Lord, just let him wave and pass by.' But he stopped dead in front of me with his hand outstretched, saying, 'Hello, I'm Jay. Would you like me to carry your pack?' My mind screamed yes, but my lips uttered, 'No, thanks. I'm okay.' My pride was totally opposed to accepting help. He turned, and we climbed together. When Jay continued to ask if he could carry my load, I finally relented.

I had prayed for strength, but God had something else in mind. Sometimes receiving God's provision requires a sacrifice on our part, like giving up our self-reliance. This sacrifice is not for God's benefit but for our own. When we are no longer distracted, burdened with guilt or full of pride, our ears and hearts are more open to God. Then we are free to sense his message in the words of a song, see his plan in the created world or feel an unexplained peace deep within us during a crisis.

Prayer: *Dear God, help us to release our pride so that we may trust in your provision rather than our own. Amen*

Thought for the day: Today I will set down my burdens so that I can welcome God's strength.

A. Mattingly (Texas, US)

God wants what is best for us

Read Hebrews 12:4–11

Endure hardship as discipline; God is treating you as his children. For what children are not disciplined by their father?
Hebrews 12:7 (NIV)

Drinking soft drinks or sweetened juice in my young nephew's presence will probably make him upset; he also likes such drinks, but because of a medical condition he is not allowed to have sugar. One day as he was crying for a drink of juice, it occurred to me that while children may cry for something that will harm them, adults who know better will allow them to cry rather than to satisfy them with what is harmful.

God called my attention to the same thing about myself. At times when I would ask God for things and not get them when I expected, I would start crying. Still, my tears didn't make God give me what I cried for. Eventually I realised the truth of Hebrews 12:7, that as a good father, God will discipline me so that I can grow. God was not denying me love by withholding certain things from me. By not giving me what I wanted, he may have been protecting me or helping me to grow and mature.

When our desires and tears are for what isn't the best, God will help us not to destroy ourselves with these misguided desires but instead to make better choices. He loves us and wants only the very best for us.

Prayer: *Dear Father, when we cry for unnecessary or harmful things, teach us to understand your discipline and embrace a love for your correction. Amen*

Thought for the day: God sees beyond what I want to what is best for me.

Oluwasola Jegede (Lagos, Nigeria)

Ourselves or others?

Read Luke 10:29–37

You do well if you really fulfil the royal law according to the scripture, 'You shall love your neighbour as yourself.'
James 2:8 (NRSV)

I was teaching English as a second language to students who were preparing to enter a university in the US. One day the class was learning to use the reflexive pronouns (myself, yourself, himself, etc.), and the students were practising by filling in the blanks in sentences in their workbooks. The sentence 'God helps those who help _____' confused one of my students. When he came up after class to ask me for the answer, I told him that this saying is common in the US and that the correct answer is 'themselves' – 'God helps those who help *themselves.*' 'Oh,' he said. 'I thought God helps those who help *others.*'

He was right. Jesus gave us two commandments that are the most important – to love God with all our heart, soul, mind and strength and to love our neighbours as ourselves (see Mark 12:28–31). The parable in today's reading also reminds us that our neighbour is anyone we meet whom we have the ability to help.

My student's response was closer to the biblical teaching than that popular saying. Even if our material resources are limited, we can offer a smile, a word of encouragement or a listening ear to those we come in contact with today. And in doing so, we also will be blessed.

Prayer: *Dear God, help us to honour you by helping someone who needs what we can give. Amen*

Thought for the day: To whom is God calling me to be a neighbour today?

Frances K. Griffin (Oklahoma, US)

'I am still here'

Read Psalm 145:1–9

So shall my word be that goes out from my mouth; it shall not return to me empty, but it shall accomplish that which I purpose.
Isaiah 55:11 (NRSV)

My husband and I needed some work done on our home, so we selected a workman to do the job. When the man came to the house, he proved to be very professional. His bid was reasonable, and we liked the fact that he was soft-spoken and kind.

As he was leaving, he said, 'I'll get back to you in a few days. I'm moving a bit slowly; I have cancer.' I was speechless.

'Actually,' he said, 'four years ago when they found the cancer, the doctor said I was a dead man; he gave me 30 days to live. I said, "I can't go yet. I have things I need to do." So I am still here.'

'Four years!' I exclaimed. 'Well,' he said with a smile, 'I am a child of God. I have people praying for me. My tumour had completely disappeared. But now it's back.' And he shrugged.

'We will keep you in our thoughts and prayers,' I said, and I took his hand as he turned to leave.

Months later, long after he had finished the work, his testimony stayed with me: 'I am a child of God.' How easily he shared his faith! With only a few words he witnessed to me, and he has inspired me to do the same with others.

Prayer: *Dear God, help us to share the good news of Christ, knowing that even simple words of witness can make a difference in the lives of people we meet. Amen*

Thought for the day: I am a child of God.

Ann Vernon (Missouri, US)

Heavy cost

Read John 3:1–21

God so loved the world that he gave his one and only Son, that whoever believes in him shall not perish but have eternal life.
John 3:16 (NIV)

Recently my son required corrective surgery for which the surgeon had to break his jaw in seven places. We knew the surgery was needed, but that only slightly reduced the stress. In a quiet corner of the surgical ward, we prayed.

'Are you scared, son?' I asked him. 'Yes,' he replied, weeping. 'I am too,' I replied.

I hugged him and prayed aloud as we turned the operation over to God – and into the hands of the surgeons and doctors. I felt helpless and wished I could have spared my son the drastic and painful procedure, but I knew that something beneficial would result from his suffering.

I couldn't help but think what it must have been like for God to watch as people purposely harmed Jesus. Certainly, God knew that the separation and suffering that Jesus endured was for the greater good. But it was not without a heavy cost.

When we look at the crucifixion, we recognise Christ's torture and death; but how often do we sense the great chasm of separation between the Son and the Father because of our sin? Seeing just that small glimpse into the Father's experience on the day of my son's surgery helped me to feel even more strongly the love God has for me.

Prayer: *Dear Lord, help us never to forget the sacrifice that you and Jesus made for our salvation. Amen*

Thought for the day: Jesus endured separation from God to separate me from my sin.

Dave Trouten (New Brunswick, Canada)

Words and actions

Read 1 Thessalonians 1:2–10

Because we loved you so much, we were delighted to share with you not only the gospel of God but our lives as well.
1 Thessalonians 2:8 (NIV)

When I married Bill, classical music was not a genre that I wanted to listen to. But it was Bill's favourite. When a classical radio station began broadcasting in our area, we tuned our alarm radio to it and awoke to classical music every weekday morning. We attended concerts and recitals, even operas, especially after our daughter became a singer. Reflecting on 48 years of marriage, I realise that Bill never insisted that I listen to classical music or argued that it was better than any other kind of music. He just listened to the music he loved, and I came to love it too.

That insight brought this thought: instead of debating about faith or insisting that others live up to my Christian values, I should live my faith trying to be kind and loving like Jesus, treating people with respect and dignity. In this way, when I do have the opportunity to tell someone, 'God loves you', they can believe me because they have seen the truth of it in my words and actions. I will be sharing the God I love in the way that Jesus did.

Prayer: *Holy God, help us to treat everyone as Jesus would treat them, so they will know through our words and actions that God loves them. Amen*

Thought for the day: How does the way I treat others encourage them to believe that God loves them?

Lin Tranter (Ohio, US)

Letting go

Read 1 Samuel 1

I prayed for this child, and the Lord has granted me what I asked of him. So now I give him to the Lord.
1 Samuel 1:27–28 (NIV)

Shortly after I was born, my mother fell ill. Her doctor prescribed strong medication that severely impaired Mum's ability to focus. But this didn't stop her from sharing Christ with me, encouraging me in my studies and cheering me on when I played sport. In spite of her pain and debilitating condition, she reached out to me with a love that nourished me spiritually, physically and emotionally. When the time came for me to leave home, it was difficult for Mum. But she trusted that God would guide me in the way I should go.

Of all the mothers in the Bible, Hannah is perhaps the best example of reaching out and then letting go. When she cried out to God, he blessed her with a baby boy, Samuel. In gratitude, Hannah kept her commitment to devote her son to God's service. Though she loved Samuel, she was willing to step aside and let the boy grow with God.

Hannah showed her devoted and sacrificial love both in her strong desire to have a child and in her willingness to give the child to God's work. Hannah is an example to us of a love that supports and also lets go.

Prayer: *Faithful God, help us to support those we love in their service to you. Amen*

Thought for the day: I can entrust those I love to God.

Tony Roberts (Indiana, US)

The right road

Read Psalm 25:4–10

I will instruct you and teach you in the way you should go.
Psalm 32:8 (NIV)

I was alone in my car driving home at night when suddenly I found myself in an area I did not recognise. I had taken the wrong road and was in a place totally unfamiliar to me. My uncertainty and anxiety at that moment were disconcerting to say the least. At last, I spotted a tall building I recognised, and it served as a point of reference. I got my bearings and found the road that would lead me home.

This experience reminds me of those who have taken the wrong road spiritually and simply wander aimlessly through life. Many of us have taken a sometimes alluring road, but such roads do not lead to a joyful destination because they lead away from God. As we travel along them, it may appear as though we know where we are headed. But our lives are often burdened with uncertainty and anxiety because we are disoriented – not even aware of our final destination.

Jesus is 'the way and the truth and the life' (John 14:6). With his help we can find the right road and help others do the same.

Prayer: *Guardian of us all, please forgive our wandering ways. We lean on you to show us the path that leads to joyful obedience and to eternal life in Jesus Christ. Amen*

Thought for the day: I will never be lost when I follow God's way.

Nelly R. Reina (Córdoba, Argentina)

Trusting God

Read James 1:2–12

Consider it pure joy, my brothers and sisters, whenever you face trials of many kinds.
James 1:2 (NIV)

During my teenage years, my greatest suffering was loneliness. Year after year, I prayed for deep Christian friendships. But year after year, God answered, 'Not yet', and I wondered why. Hadn't I put effort into finding friendships? Wouldn't godly friendships help me grow in my relationship with God? Wasn't strong Christian fellowship a part of God's plan?

The book of James tells us to consider sufferings as joy because suffering strengthens and matures us into who God calls us to be. While I was alone during my teenage years, I learned to depend on God and to empathise with and reach out to those who were unpopular. I learned to value and strengthen the relationships I already had, especially with my brothers and sisters. Lastly, being alone – reading and thinking – moved me to put those thoughts on paper and gave me the courage to share my writing with others.

God does not tell us that suffering is joyful. Suffering is suffering, and the loneliness I experienced was not in itself a good thing. Still, God tells us to 'consider it pure joy'. Now, I can consider that loneliness as joy because of what God has brought about through it.

Prayer: *Dear Lord, through whatever we are suffering today, help us to find joy in trusting you so that we may learn to persevere and become more like Jesus. Amen*

Thought for the day: Even in my suffering I can persevere in trusting God.

Tim Pietz (Wisconsin, US)

Faith in God's word

Read Psalm 23

Yea, though I walk through the valley of the shadow of death, I will fear no evil: for thou art with me; thy rod and thy staff they comfort me.

Psalm 23:4 (KJV)

In April 1980 my family was caught in a deadly military overthrow of the government. As we took cover from the rapid fire of machine guns on our Liberian home, we recited Psalm 23 repeatedly. I recall reciting today's verse countless times as the gunfire drowned out our voices. The soldiers shot at the house nonstop for 25 minutes. I knew that my family and I might perish, but I remained focused on my faith.

The soldiers shot the back door down, and I heard the thud of their boots as they entered the house. They finally found us on the floor in the bedroom. I prayed quietly and asked God to save us. My prayer was formed out of the definition of faith in Hebrews 11:1: 'Faith is confidence in what we hope for and assurance about what we do not see' (NIV). God did not speak to me personally that day, but my faith was all I had. When it was all over, I knew how powerful faith in God and his word can be.

I continue to read this psalm to my children, my grandchildren and the women whom I counsel in my work. Whenever I find myself facing a crisis, I turn to the fourth verse of Psalm 23. No matter how grave our problem, the Lord will keep us close and give us comfort.

Prayer: *Dear Father in heaven, teach us to stay close to you and to strengthen our faith in your presence. Amen*

Thought for the day: When danger is present, the power of God's word prevails.

Angela Peabody (Virginia, US)

Whatever we do

Read Colossians 3:15–17

Whatever you do, whether in word or deed, do it all in the name of the Lord Jesus, giving thanks to God the Father through him.
Colossians 3:17 (NIV)

In January 1959 I was a relatively new Christian when I arrived for my new posting at Osan Air Force Base in South Korea. As an airman second class I had two stripes on my sleeve. The sergeant who was also checking in had five, showing that he outranked me. When he used some swear words within earshot of the Korean woman who was handling our paperwork, I quietly asked him to be careful of his language. I could tell he did not take my suggestion very well. When we got outside, the sergeant angrily lashed out at me and said that if he became my boss I would be in big trouble. When he became the sergeant over me, he carried out his threat by assigning me a severely damaged plane.

I was determined that no matter how he treated me or how frustrating my assignment, I would repair that plane 'as unto Christ' (Ephesians 6:5, KJV.) My faith helped me to do everything the sergeant asked me to do without complaining and with a positive attitude. After weeks of hard work, the plane I had repaired passed a test flight with no problems. That August, because the sergeant had been so impressed by my work, he nominated me to be airman of the month.

It is always best when we put Christ first in any situation and trust the outcome to God.

Prayer: *Dear Lord, help us not to be intimidated by others so that we can live out our Christian faith wherever we are. Amen*

Thought for the day: I will follow Christ no matter what the circumstances are.

Gordon B. Rose (Indiana, US)

'I trust you'

Read Psalm 29

Look at the birds of the air; they do not sow or reap or store away in barns, and yet your heavenly Father feeds them. Are you not much more valuable than they?
Matthew 6:26 (NIV)

When I was injured in an accident and had concussion, I wasn't able to care for my young son or maintain a conversation with my husband for quite some time. I could do no housework; I couldn't go to church; I wasn't able to read my Bible. Even praying was difficult. Although God surrounded me with many wonderful people who helped immensely during this time, I still felt cut off from the world and very much alone.

I will never forget one beautiful spring day when I was sitting in our garden. Suddenly I could feel God all around me – in the warmth of the sunshine, in the gentle breeze and through the singing of the birds. When I heard them, the verse above came to me. It seemed as if God were saying, 'Give up all your fears, tears and anxieties and just trust me.' It still took another three months before I could read my Bible or have a normal conversation. But every time I broke down crying or felt as if I couldn't handle the stress any more, I would stop myself and say aloud, 'I trust you, God!'

Life has many battles, some larger than others, but God is with us. We can acknowledge that his ways are greater than ours. Surrendering our lives to the Lord our God, we can say, 'I trust you!'

Prayer: *Dear God, forgive us when we try to handle our difficulties all on our own. Help us to turn to you for guidance, wisdom and strength. Amen*

Thought for the day: Today and every day I will tell God, 'I trust you!'

Ashley Swartzentruber (Ontario, Canada)

See the face of God

Read Genesis 33:1–11

'Please!' said Jacob. 'If I have found favour in your eyes, accept this gift from me. For to see your face is like seeing the face of God.'
Genesis 33:10 (NIV)

Growing up, I was no saint – any more than Esau. My younger brother was not a devil – any more than Jacob. Like all siblings, we competed for time, affection and family resources. For a while, almost every day when we arrived home from school, I would so frustrate my younger brother that he would start fights with me. Looking back, I realise that if the shoe had been on the other foot, I'd probably have done just as my brother did.

When my brother recently wrote to me for perhaps the third time expressing regret for his behaviour in our younger years, I was finally mature enough to see what he had long needed from me. He needed the face of God looking back at him saying, 'Forget about it. It's finished; it's over.' Neither of us was an angel, so certainly he isn't the only one who needed to apologise.

As if scales had fallen from my eyes, I realised I needed to assure my brother that he is forgiven and that his reaching out to me helped me to move on. He was doing all the heavy lifting. Until we've asked for forgiveness from another, we can't imagine the sense of God's glory that comes when we extend ourselves this way in love.

Prayer: *Dear God, thank you for showing us how to forgive and for allowing us to see your glory when we do. Amen*

Thought for the day: When I ask for forgiveness, I have a chance to see the face of God.

Jack Stanley (Florida, US)

Answers to prayer

Read Matthew 7:7–12

How much more will your Father in heaven give good gifts to those who ask him!
Matthew 7:11 (NIV)

It was a perfect day for a picnic. Tourists sauntered into the shade of the valley to stretch out on the grass, where trees offered shade from the sun. It was getting hot. Overhead a flock of seagulls circled, waiting for the first crumbs to fall. Close by, a man spread a blanket on the ground before peering into a green bag to retrieve his lunch.

My throat was parched. Why hadn't I thought to bring lunch with me? I watched a little enviously as he dipped into the bag, a look of anticipation on his face. With two large hands he reached the bottom of the bag and withdrew – a tortoise! The man placed it carefully on the blanket, and it set out to explore. Nothing is ever as it seems, I thought, and the world is full of surprises.

Then I thought about my prayer life. I hope my prayers will be answered and often they are, but there have been times when I think God hasn't heard me. Perhaps these are times when God surprises me by answering my prayers in different ways. Maybe the answer is 'Yes.' Sometimes it could be 'No' or 'Not yet.'

Whatever we feel about it, we need never think that God does not hear us or that he does not answer our prayers. Knowing us as he does, he knows our every need.

Prayer: *Lord, help us to trust you with our prayers and to know always that you hear us. Amen*

Thought for the day: Today I will remember that God hears my prayers.

Pauline Pullan (Yorkshire, United Kingdom)

Seeing past the obstacles

Read Proverbs 3:5-6
We live by faith, not by sight.
2 Corinthians 5:7 (NIV)

Early one evening my friend Sherry phoned, telling me to go outside and look at the sunset. She described how beautiful the colours were and how the sky was a brilliant pink surrounding the setting sun. I eagerly went outside to look, but to my disappointment, my view was totally blocked by the trees. However, even though I couldn't see it, from my friend's vivid description and my past experiences of enjoying beautiful sunsets I could imagine how brilliant the sky looked.

So often it is the same for me as I try to live faithfully each day. When I am going through trials, it can be hard to see God at work in the situation. My eyes can be so focused on my need that I do not see an answer or the way through my struggles. But reading God's promises in scripture and my past experiences of seeing God's work in my life reassure me that God is present, even though I cannot see past the obstructions that are blocking my view. As we recall God's blessings and answers to our prayers in the past, we can trust and envision that God is at work in our lives.

Prayer: *Creator God, help us to remember your answers to prayers and trust that you are at work in our lives. Amen*

Thought for the day: Even when I cannot see God's presence, God is working in my life.

Monabeth Milliron (Louisiana, US)

Loved so much

Read Romans 8:31–39

There is no fear in love. But perfect love drives out fear, because fear has to do with punishment. The one who fears is not made perfect in love. We love because [God] first loved us.
1 John 4:18–19 (NIV)

Almost seven years ago, our first grandson, Zachary, was born on the other side of the world. He suffered brain damage at birth and could barely breathe on his own. Zachary's parents spent every moment they could with him during his twelve-hour life, and we were all devastated when he died.

I asked myself, 'What did this baby do to deserve all this love? Was he good or clever? Did he help others?' But Zachary did none of these things. His parents loved him so much and always will because he was their son. They would have moved heaven and earth to save him and to keep him with them if they could.

In those difficult days, I realised that God loves me not for anything I have done or can do but just because I am his child. God did move heaven and earth by sending his Son, so that we can be with him forever.

I have always struggled to believe in my heart that God loves me. Zachary helped me to understand.

Prayer: *Dear God, help us to rest in your love and to know that we don't have to earn it. Thank you for loving us as your children. Amen*

Thought for the day: God loves me and wants to be near me forever.

Jenny Young (Gauteng, South Africa)

The first place

Read Psalm 34:4–7

[The Lord] refreshes my soul.
Psalm 23:3 (NIV)

When I was eight years old, I remember helping my father search for his lost keys. As his frustration mounted, he asked, 'Why is it that whenever you lose something, it's always in the last place you look?' With a grin, he then added, 'Because once you find it, you stop looking.' I thought this was a hilarious observation. From that moment forward, finding lost items became a game for me. My goal was that the first place I looked should be the last.

This approach is fine for trivial items, such as shoes, sunglasses or the remote control. But where do we look when we lose courage, hope or direction? Where do we look when we lose ourselves? In times of need, it's far too common to look for answers in all the wrong places. Seeking relief, we may turn to alcohol, drugs or other unhealthy behaviour, none of which help us to find anything good.

Scripture reminds us that in our most trying times, we can look to God first for help and solace. As our provider, God can restore, renew and replenish us. Prayer allows us to seek God's counsel, and scripture allows us to rediscover God's endless love, which can rebuild our broken spirits. At some point in our lives, we all experience significant loss. It's comforting to know exactly where to look to regain our strength and stability.

Prayer: *Dear Lord, thank you for being an ever-present force in our lives. Help us to remember that we can always seek you in times of need. Amen*

Thought for the day: For life's biggest problems, I will first look to God for answers.

Webb Smith (Georgia, US)

Everyday opportunities

Read Acts 26:12–18

[Jesus] said to them, 'Go into all the world and proclaim the good news to the whole creation.'
Mark 16:15 (NRSV)

Despite our phone number being ex-directory, my husband and I still receive a number of irritating sales calls each day. One day, my husband said, 'What if we used these calls to reach out to those who don't know Jesus?' After praying about it, we decided to tell callers that we'd listen to their spiel but that we wanted to say something to them first.

We ask the callers whether they have a relationship with Jesus, and we discuss God's saving grace and the gift of salvation. Sometimes we ask the caller whether there is something we can pray for on their behalf. Occasionally we are met with coldness, but we more often have genuine conversations with people across the world. We then patiently listen to the reason for their call and thank them for the opportunity to talk to them.

Through these conversations we know we've planted the seed of God's love, and we pray that the Holy Spirit will guide them forward. It's amazing how God turned our annoyance into a way to share the good news with others all over the world!

Prayer: *Heavenly Father, help us to be open to opportunities to share your love. May your Holy Spirit cause the seeds we sow to grow and multiply so that others may find eternal life. Amen*

Thought for the day: Unexpected encounters can be opportunities to show God's love.

Carolyn Strickland (Florida, US)

One by one

Read John 1:35–50

Day by day the Lord added to their number those who were being saved.

Acts 2:47 (NRSV)

Since my early mathematics classes, I have been intrigued by the number one. By itself, it is weak and powerless. Even when it is multiplied by itself, it retains the same value. But in its relationship with other numbers, it becomes powerful. Even the greatest number increases when this small number is added to it, and when a critical decision has to be voted on, one vote can make all the difference.

I find this to be an important comment on Christian life and the growth of the church. When I look at the first church, I notice that its growth is not spoken of as multiplication but rather addition. The gospels tell us how Jesus called his disciples personally, one by one, and their number grew as each responded to Jesus' invitation to follow him. When each of us follows Jesus, we are given the grace to contribute to the growth of God's kingdom.

Prayer: *Dear God, thank you for adding each of us to your kingdom so that we may live in fellowship with you and with all your people. As Jesus taught us, we pray, 'Our Father in heaven, hallowed be your name, your kingdom come, your will be done, on earth as it is in heaven. Give us today our daily bread. And forgive us our debts, as we also have forgiven our debtors. And lead us not into temptation, but deliver us from the evil one.'* Amen*

Thought for the day: In God's kingdom, I am never alone.

Colin D. Harbach (Cumbria, United Kingdom)

PRAYER FOCUS: MATHEMATICS TEACHERS
*Matthew 6:9–13 (NIV)

Guide my prayers

Read Romans 8:25–28

The Spirit helps us in our weakness. We do not know what we ought to pray for, but the Spirit himself intercedes for us through wordless groans.

Romans 8:26 (NIV)

'This one's a firecracker!' the paediatrician said when my husband and I took our first child for her one-year checkup. Extroverted and confident, Madison has lived up to that description ever since. Her little sister, Anna, is different. If someone outside our immediate family talked to Anna when she was younger, she would lower her gaze and bury her face in my neck. Concerned about Anna's shyness, I asked my Bible study group to pray for her to come out of her shell. Some wise, experienced mothers advised me that Anna would eventually find her way in the world on her own terms.

Then I realised that I had been praying for the wrong thing – focusing on what would make me comfortable instead of what made Anna comfortable. Rather than praying for God to change Anna, I should have been praying for God to change me.

When I changed my prayers, my stress over Anna's shyness lifted. At the age of nine, Anna surprised everyone when she began acting and singing, and she continued these activities throughout her school days. God had worked through the Holy Spirit – and my wise friends – to guide my prayers to help me let Anna be Anna.

Prayer: *Dear Lord, help us to listen for the Holy Spirit's guidance to put our prayers on the right track. Amen*

Thought for the day: When I listen to the Holy Spirit, my prayers can more fully follow God's will.

Marcy Farr (Texas, US)

A loving embrace

Read Psalm 103:13–18

These three remain: faith, hope and love. But the greatest of these is love.
1 Corinthians 13:13 (NIV)

When I was 14 years old, my father was in a serious car accident and suffered a traumatic brain injury. Some days he could barely walk because he was in severe pain. His recovery took ten years. This was a difficult time for my family, since our main breadwinner could no longer work. Life changed for all of us.

One night when I was 16, my dad was in his room alone. For some reason, I thought that I should show him how much I loved him. I believe now that God directed me. I walked into his room, told him that I loved him and embraced him. I held my father for several minutes, and tears rolled down his cheeks. At the time, I didn't know what I had done for him. I didn't know the pain and depression he was going through, the worthlessness he felt or that he was feeling tempted by thoughts of suicide. To this day, my dad cherishes that embrace and thanks me for it.

Over the years, my dad and I have told many others about that special moment. We may never know the full impact of that one embrace. God showed me that even the smallest act of love can change a life forever.

Prayer: *Heavenly Father, thank you for loving us as your children. Guide us to show love to those who need it. Amen*

Thought for the day: What sign of love is God prompting me to show?

David Smith (US)

Rescued and sustained

Read Isaiah 46:3–4

Even to your old age and grey hairs I am he, I am he who will sustain you. I have made you and I will carry you; I will sustain you and I will rescue you.
Isaiah 46:4 (NIV)

A few years ago, a plant sprouted near the patio of our house. We didn't know what kind of plant it was, but as it grew higher it looked as if it were going to grow into a tree. My father planned to cut it down because he didn't want it to block the light to the house. However, when he learned I liked the plant, he let it grow.

A few weeks later, I noticed that the stem of the plant had cracked. Strong winds must have damaged it during the night. I phoned my sister and told her how sad I was. To my surprise, she came to the house, took some string and tied the stem of the plant to a nail on the wall. After some time the plant has grown into a fairly tall tree.

In life, like the stem of that plant, we often find ourselves 'cracked'. Heavy burdens, such as financial problems and health issues, are like the strong winds that damaged my plant. But God can sustain us like the rope supported the tree. In Isaiah 46:4, God promises to sustain us, even to our old age and grey hairs. With that promise, we can live in the peace and joy that trusting God can bring.

Prayer: *Almighty God, in every problem help us to trust that your strength will sustain us. Amen*

Thought for the day: When I feel weak, I can rely on God's strength to sustain me.

Linawati Santoso (East Java, Indonesia)

By our side

Read John 11:32–44

Jesus began to weep.
John 11:35 (NRSV)

As I write this meditation, it is exactly 34 years since my mother and I stood by my father's hospital bed to say our final goodbyes. Even after all these years I still miss him. Although I was feeling my own personal pain, it was my privilege as an only child to stand by my mother's side in her deep grief over losing her husband of 43 years. As much as I wanted to, I could not take away her sadness; it was something that she had to work through in her own way.

At times like these, nothing we say can make all the pain go away. Sometimes just being present – as hard as that may be – is enough. I learned this over the 25 years that I was an intensive-care chaplain serving grieving families, by offering my presence, my comfort and my prayers. But the sense of God's presence with us really makes all the difference. Today's quoted verse opens us to the sacred heart of our Lord. God is touched by the pain we feel and is present to comfort us. Jesus' presence made all the difference for Mary and Martha. Still today, when we stand with one another in grief, it can make all the difference for us as well.

Prayer: *Living God, give us the courage and love to be present with those who are grieving and to be channels of your comfort to those who are hurting. Amen*

Thought for the day: God is with me in my joys and in my sorrows.

J. Leland Collins, Jr (Virginia, US)

Hope

Read Psalm 103:1–12

I will rejoice in the Lord, I will be joyful in God my Saviour.
Habakkuk 3:18 (NIV)

In 2001, my husband was diagnosed with cancer, my uncle died and my mother's congestive heart failure took a turn for the worse. A few months later my husband began cancer treatment, his father passed away unexpectedly and my mother died.

Memories of the traumatic events of that year make it easy to overlook the positive things that happened. During those painful times, grief was a natural response. But I had to choose whether to remain bitter, angry and discouraged or, like the prophet Habakkuk, to say, 'Yet I will rejoice in the Lord.'

We all experience circumstances that leave us reeling and wondering which way to turn and if we will survive. Tough times are often beyond our control, but we can still choose how we react to the events. Psalm 103 reminds us to praise God because he is gracious, forgiving, compassionate and abounding in love. Even when we do not understand how any good can possibly come from our present circumstances, we can choose whether we will focus on the negative or the blessings God has given us.

Prayer: *Dear God, help us to choose to praise you every day, regardless of our circumstances. Amen*

Thought for the day: Today and every day, I will be joyful in God.

Carol Elaine Harrison (Saskatchewan, Canada)

Would I do the same?

Read Mark 5:1–20

Those who had actually seen what had happened to the demon-possessed man told the others about the pigs. Then they pleaded with Jesus to leave their region.

Mark 5:16–17 (CEB)

Each time I read today's verse I find myself in stunned disbelief. Despite another wonderful and amazing miracle, the crowd still didn't want to accept Jesus and emphatically asked him to leave. In the past, reading these verses often led me to wonder, 'Why would they want Jesus to leave when he had healed a demon-possessed man and cast out a legion of evil spirits? Why would they reject the presence of Christ?'

Recently, as I read these verses I had a different question. This time I asked myself, 'Would I ever do the same?' I realised that at times I too ask Jesus to leave me. When I choose anger and hateful speech, choose my ways over God's commands, choose to misrepresent the truth or choose to stand quiet when I should speak out, I'm rejecting Jesus.

The people may have rejected Jesus, but the demon-possessed man, now fully rational, was the one who got it right. He knew that Jesus was someone to follow and stay near. May we too learn not to send Christ away but instead to follow him steadfastly.

Prayer: *Dear Lord, forgive us when we choose paths that separate us from you. Instead, help us choose paths of grace and love. Amen*

Thought for the day: Every day, I will seek ways to draw near to God.

Cassius Rhue (South Carolina, US)

Living covering letter

Read 2 Corinthians 3:1–6

You show that you are a letter from Christ, the result of our ministry, written not with ink but with the Spirit of the living God, not on tablets of stone but on tablets of human hearts.
2 Corinthians 3:3 (NIV)

I struggled to write a covering letter to accompany an article I was submitting to a magazine. The editor required the letter as a way of introducing myself. But did listing facts such as my educational background, job experiences and previous publications allow the editor to really know me? He would know about me from reading my letter, but knowing about me is not the same as knowing me. Only by spending time with me, listening to my words and observing my actions, would the editor really know who I am.

Christians are living covering letters for Christ. Every day we write a letter for those around us to read. We can tell others about Christ by listing various facts: he was a great teacher, he healed the sick and he was crucified and raised to new life. But knowing things about Christ does not mean that we know who he is. As living covering letters, Christians convey who Christ is. Then others may come to know Christ by spending time with us and observing our earthly reflection of our heavenly Saviour. Will those we encounter come to know Christ by our living letter?

Prayer: *Living Lord, help us to reflect you in our words and actions each day so that others may desire to know and serve you fully. Amen*

Thought for the day: How will I be a living letter for Christ today?

Alice H. Murray (Florida, US)

A cry for help

Read Psalm 91

I cried unto the Lord with my voice, and he heard me out of his holy hill.

Psalm 3:4 (KJV)

I had been driving to a town almost 200 miles away for an annual conference. I had set out expecting the drive to be enjoyable, but then my car broke down. With no emergency roadside help available, I phoned some colleagues who were attending the same conference. Somehow, they passed by me and had to turn back to find me. It was getting dark; the situation was looking bleak and I was getting scared. I uttered a desperate prayer, 'Help me, Lord!' My colleagues finally found me and the story ended well.

So many times we find ourselves in bad situations, jumping into things without careful consideration or proper planning. We hope that everything will sort itself out. Often, by the time we realise our errors, we have already reached the point of no return.

Thankfully God does not care for us according to our faithfulness or intelligence but according to his unconditional love and tender mercies. No matter how bleak the situation, God is only a prayer away. The eloquence of our prayers does not matter; a desperate cry from a needy heart is enough to catch God's attention.

Prayer: *Dear Lord, remind us of your promise never to leave us or forsake us. Help us to turn to you – especially in threatening circumstances. Amen*

Thought for the day: No situation is so dark that God cannot find and help me.

Demi Oyinloye (Ogun, Nigeria)

Smothering the ball

I started playing golf a few years ago. Though frustrating at times, it can also be an exceedingly rewarding sport. Each bad shot is nothing compared to the exhilaration of a good one, the ball landing precisely where you aimed. My first few times on the driving range were spent missing the ball entirely and digging up grass and soil instead. If I was lucky enough to hit the ball, it was anyone's guess where it would go.

In an effort to improve my game, I started taking lessons. My instructor repeatedly told me that I was smothering the ball. I was trying so hard to control the ball that I would clench my muscles and contort my body in strange ways, leaving no room for the club to do its work. As a result, nine times out of ten my shot fell flat. It was only after I learned to relax and trust the club that I started hitting better shots.

The way I approach my golf game has taught me a lot about myself. I 'smother the ball' in many aspects of my life. I try so hard to control – even force – the outcome of some situations that I leave no room for God to work. And I usually end up making matters worse. However, I am beginning to understand more and more that part of having a relationship with God is knowing when to let go. It's having the wisdom to leave room for God to do what he does best – work for my good.

Scripture is full of people who gave up control in order to allow God to work in their lives and in the lives of his people: Noah, Moses, Joshua, Ruth, Jonah, Mary, the first disciples. Moses helped to deliver the Israelites from captivity. Joshua led God's people across the Jordan and into Canaan. Jonah finally went to Nineveh. Each shows us the value of trust in God over our own limited abilities.

Throughout scripture we see how much God loves us and that he wants only the best for us. But this means that sometimes we have to set aside our own concerns, fears and ideas so that God can work. Noah followed God's command to build an ark – though without a drop of water in sight surely he looked silly doing it. Hannah gave Samuel to the Lord as she had promised, in spite of how difficult it must have been to let go of the son she loved so much. Such trust does not always come naturally to me.

One of the hardest lessons that I have had to learn – one that I am still in the process of learning – is that my ability to control many situations only goes so far. And in some cases it doesn't go far at all. In such times, letting go is easier said than done; it requires practice and discipline, not to mention obedience and confidence in God. It is hard for me to imagine the courage it must have taken for Joshua to lead the Israelites into the promised land or the fear Jonah must have felt in the belly of the fish. Both Joshua and Jonah, however, ultimately set aside their own concerns so that God could work. In my golf game, I have constantly to tell myself to remain calm when making a shot. I remind myself to trust the club to finish the job, and then take my shot. When I do, the outcome is much better. The same is true when I am in a challenging work situation, having a difficult relationship with a friend or colleague or struggling to make a decision. Putting more confidence and trust in God and less in my own abilities can make all the difference.

Several meditations in this issue address trusting in God. You may want to read again the meditations for May 13, 15, 28; June 6, 9, 19, 23; July 9, 17; August 4, 7, 10, 15 and 31 before responding to the reflection questions below.

QUESTIONS FOR REFLECTION

1 When has it been difficult for you to let go of your trust in your own strength? What were your prayers like during this time? Why can it be so hard to let go?

2 Reflect on characters in scripture who were reluctant to accept God's help. Why were they reluctant? How does their story end? In that situation, what would you have done differently?

3 Name three places in your life where you see God working for your good.

Andrew Garland Breeden
Acquisitions Editor

God's handwriting

Read Psalm 19:1–4

The heavens declare the glory of God; the skies proclaim the work of his hands.

Psalm 19:1 (NIV)

I am especially glad when the postie delivers a letter, and I see the handwriting of a dear friend or family member. I don't need to open the envelope to know who wrote the letter; I recognise the author by their handwriting. My college friend's handwriting is round and enthusiastic. My childhood friend's handwriting is bold and flowery. My mother has the practised handwriting of a teacher. Their written words are concrete reflections of themselves. Because I know them so well, I can recognise their handwriting anywhere.

God's creation and work in our lives also bear an unmistakable mark. The strokes of God's hand reflect who he is. David affirms this in today's reading and quoted scripture verse. In Romans, Paul notes: 'Since the creation of the world God's invisible qualities – his eternal power and divine nature – have been clearly seen, being understood from what has been made' (Romans 1:20). God's signature is clear to all who look for it.

My friends' handwriting is familiar to me because I know them so well. And the better we come to know God through scripture, prayer and daily meditation, the more we can recognise his handiwork in the world and in our lives.

Prayer: *Creator God, open our eyes to see your unmistakable mark on all that you have done so that we may understand you more fully. Amen*

Thought for the day: Where do I see the strokes of God's hand today?

Suzanne Felton (Virginia, US)

Unending love

Read Job 42:10–13

After Job had prayed for his friends, the Lord restored his fortunes and gave him twice as much as he had before.

Job 42:10 (NIV)

Not long after I turned 40, my health started going downhill. I had no appetite, and I struggled with sleeplessness, weight loss and irrational thinking. My marriage was in trouble, and our oldest child was leaving for university. I had always been able to fix most things fairly easily, but this was different. During my darkest moments my thoughts turned to Job and the suffering he endured. Job didn't rebuke God but held on to his faith. In the end, all was restored to him.

During the depth of my suffering, Job's story gave me hope that I too would come through this valley. Finally, after a couple of months, and still suffering from weight loss and sleeplessness, I was sent to hospital. The diagnosis was severe clinical depression. The pain I felt both physically and emotionally was extreme. But with the right medication and a caring medical team I started to improve. My appetite returned and I slept well. After ten days in the hospital I was discharged.

The story of Job's suffering and restoration were key parts of my recovery. Though at times it may feel as if God has abandoned us, if we hold on to our faith, his love will carry us through the darkest of days. It has been 30 years since my diagnosis, and every day I give thanks for the story of Job and the way he never turned away from God's unending love.

Prayer: *Dear Lord, through our darkest and brightest days we give thanks for your unending love for us. Amen*

Thought for the day: God's love will carry me through my darkest days.

Larry Dowell (North Carolina, US)

Taking out the rubbish

Read Romans 6:1–13

Do not let sin reign in your mortal body so that you obey its evil desires.
Romans 6:12 (NIV)

Working in the unforgiving heat of the day during our clean-up campaign, approximately 70 people were busy cleaning a contaminated mangrove swamp. When we took a short break, I asked Nicolás, a young man on our team, how this experience had been for him. 'At first it was just gross,' he replied. 'But as I got used to the smell and surroundings, I was able to pick up even the most disgusting things. In a way, this rubbish around us is like the sin in my heart.'

His comment reminded me of how easily we become accustomed to our own sin or wrongdoing. When sin makes us uncomfortable, we are disgusted. However, doing nothing about it seems to lessen its impact on our conscience. In the end, we become accustomed to living with it or spend the rest of our lives complaining about it – convinced that we cannot confront it. Nicolás' assessment is a clear reminder that it is time to remove the rubbish and clutter from our hearts and to seek refuge in Christ, who can redeem us from sin and refresh our spirits.

Prayer: *God, our maker and friend, create in us a clean spirit and a willingness to attune our hearts to live in the light of your truth. Amen*

Thought for the day: I want to notice and repent of my sins so that I may honour God.

Perla Iveth Murillo Zapata (Colombia)

The widow's offering

Read Mark 12:41–44

Truly I tell you, this poor widow has put in more than all those who are contributing to the treasury.
Mark 12:43 (NRSV)

As a young sailor disembarking from the USS *Newport News* to tour the old brick streets of Lisbon, Portugal, I saw an old man in dirty clothing begging on the kerb. I did not understand Portuguese, but his gestures were clear. My heart was touched, and I wanted to give him some money. However, I realised that the recent currency conversion of my meagre monthly salary had left me with bills larger than what I was willing to give. I went into a nearby shop to get some change and immediately went back to the pavement. The transaction could not have taken more than 15 minutes, yet the man was no longer in sight.

I felt that I had been tested and had failed. Unwilling to give abundantly, I had wanted to offer only a comfortable amount. In my mind, the man in need was an angel – not necessarily sent to test me but to teach me the true meaning of the Lord's message about giving. Sixty years later, I still remember that man and the lesson I learned. I am most thankful that even when I fail to give from the heart, the Lord still loves me and teaches me.

Prayer: *Dear Lord, thank you for your constant presence, patience and love. Help us to give generously to people in need. Amen*

Thought for the day: God is pleased when I give generously.

Allen Goins (Florida, US)

Meeting needs

Read Philippians 4:10–20

My God will meet all your needs according to the riches of his glory in Christ Jesus.
Philippians 4:19 (NIV)

Each Friday, people flock to a farmers' market near my home to buy meat, cheese, vegetables and other items. Shoppers look for different things, according to their needs.

That's just like the people who attend our churches. Some come seeking fellowship. Some seek teaching. Some come to sing; others stand mute during hymns but pray the Lord's Prayer with heartfelt emotion. Some share their gifts of teaching, leadership or encouragement. All who serve, who speak kind words to the grieving, the broken or the wounded, find their own hearts blessed through sharing. We are a diverse group; but no matter why we attend church, our needs are met by God and his people.

None of us knows the answer to every need, but we know that God does. Maybe our job is to invite friends to church so that they can begin a relationship with God and a loving community of believers.

Prayer: *Dear God, help us to value the contribution of all who attend our churches. Guide us to meet the needs of others as we seek to serve you. As Jesus taught us, we pray, 'Father, hallowed be your name, your kingdom come. Give us each day our daily bread. Forgive us our sins, for we also forgive everyone who sins against us. And lead us not into temptation.'* Amen*

Thought for the day: No need is so great that God cannot meet it.

Shirley Brosius (Pennsylvania, US)

Always near

Read Psalm 139:7–10

When I was a child, I spoke like a child, I thought like a child, I reasoned like a child; when I became an adult, I put an end to childish ways.

1 Corinthians 13:11 (NRSV)

Psychologist Jean Piaget carried out psychological experiments in which he observed that very young children (under six months old) would be clearly interested in a toy placed a few yards in front of them until Piaget placed a blanket over the toy. Then, the children showed no further interest, assuming that the toy was no longer there.

Sometimes we are like those children. We focus clearly on the Lord while in church, when at prayer, while reading the Bible and when meditating. But when such activities cease, our focus on the Lord is often directed to other affairs.

We are not alone in concluding that God has stepped out of our lives. Jonah thought that by taking a ship going in the opposite direction to Nineveh, God would no longer be in control of his life (see Jonah 1:1–10). However, this proved not to be true, and in the fullness of time Jonah did indeed come face to face with God once again.

God is still there for us and still interested in us, though we may have temporarily lost interest in him. God is always with us.

Prayer: *Dear God, help us to feel close to you not only during worship and prayer but at all times. Amen*

Thought for the day: God is always interested in me.

Bill Findlay (Scotland, United Kingdom)

Joy

Read James 1:2–6, 12–17

Consider it pure joy, my brothers and sisters, whenever you face trials of many kinds.
James 1:2 (NIV)

I grew up braving bees and thorns to pick wild blackberries for the promise of winter pies. Recently, I picked alone, leaning into the thorny branches as always. I knew the thorns would scratch my legs and arms and snag my clothes as I stretched out for the ripe, dark berries that less-dedicated pickers thought too risky to collect. But I didn't mind the scratches. In fact, I loved them. They were a reminder of my child-hood, a mark of dedication and a promise of good things to come. As I picked, God brought to mind the phrase 'joy in the midst of suffering'. I was so surprised that I stopped picking.

The Bible has much to say about suffering and how we should respond to it. By no measure have I suffered much, but I have always understood that suffering brings us closer to God, who gives us strength to endure it. Before this time I had not quite understood the concept of counting our trials as joy.

Even in minor challenges God helps to increase our understanding, and so berry picking became an unlikely lesson. Scratches are not the same as persecution, disease or death. But for me, they were a reminder. In the future I may face severe trials; but however they may sting, I can endure them with joy for the sake of the good qualities I know that God will produce in me.

Prayer: *Giver of joy, comfort our souls when we face hardships. Amen*

Thought for the day: What good thing did God put in the midst of my challenges today?

Rachel Lulich (Indiana, US)

Standing up

Read Luke 10:25–37

In everything do to others as you would have them do to you; for this is the law and the prophets.

Matthew 7:12 (NRSV)

One day at school, I saw some pupils bullying a girl in my class. They ganged up on her, saying really mean things to her. She seemed on the verge of tears. But instead of defending her, I walked away and let her fend for herself. I could have supported her, but instead I thought only of myself and decided not to get involved.

Later I thought, 'If someone were saying those mean things to me, I would have been upset and hurt. Even if someone thought about standing up for me, it would mean nothing if they just thought about it and did nothing.'

The next time the bullies made fun of her, I walked up to them and told them to stop. Some of my friends came with me to defend her. We took the girl away from the bullies and asked if she was all right. She told us that she was going through a really hard time, even having suicidal thoughts.

Eventually the bullies left her alone. Meanwhile, that girl became my good friend and slowly regained her self-respect. That day I learned that a small act, like standing up for someone, can make a huge difference for the person on the other end.

Prayer: *Dear Lord, help us to stand with others during difficult times and to treat others the way we want to be treated. Amen*

Thought for the day: God loves everyone, and I will too.

Rebecca Auger (North Carolina, US)

God's broken vessels

Read Psalm 36:5–9
The Lord is close to the broken-hearted and saves those who are crushed in spirit.
Psalm 34:18 (NIV)

I have always been fascinated by Kintsugi, the traditional Japanese art of mending broken pieces of pottery with liquid gold, silver or lacquer, thus highlighting and enhancing the breaks and adding value to the broken objects.

Kintsugi reminds me of my condition. Many times in my journey of faith I have found myself defeated and wretched, having given up hope. I was ashamed to face God. I pleaded, 'God, I want to give up. My brokenness and my sins mock me.' Then always God's voice would come in reply, 'I haven't given up on you, my dear child. Why should you give up on me?' The more broken and shattered I became, the more God's grace seemed to surround me.

My struggles have shown me that I need to trust in God's strength because my own strength can fail me. But all along my Christian journey, God has picked up and mended my pieces. Today, I am a beautiful creation of broken pieces, mended by God's love and grace.

At times, we all feel unloved, dejected or lonely. But God is greater than our brokenness. Broken lives and broken hopes are precious in the sight of God, who can use even broken vessels to carry out great plans.

Prayer: *Dear God, remind us not to give up on you when we are broken. Amen*

Thought for the day: I will not give up on God, who has never given up on me.

Wati Mollier (Nagaland, India)

Surprise guest

Read Hebrews 2:5–18

The one who makes people holy and those who are made holy are of the same family. So Jesus is not ashamed to call them brothers and sisters.

Hebrews 2:11 (NIV)

One of my earliest childhood memories is when my grandparents surprised us by arriving at our house unannounced. They lived eight hours away so we were overjoyed to see them. My grandparents had brought me a gift, but the real treat was their presence.

When Jesus was born, he arrived in a surprising way. Rather than living as a king in a palace, Jesus lived as an ordinary person. Working as a carpenter, Jesus knew the value of hard work. During his ministry, Jesus travelled long hours without a place to lay his head.

Because of the way Jesus lived, he was able to build personal relationships with many people. He shared wisdom with tax collectors and fishermen, Jews and Gentiles, men and women. Today, when we show warmth to those around us we reflect the perfect type of love that Jesus modelled.

My grandparents taught me about Jesus and the gift of his life as a human being. Jesus showed us the way to live as friends and family with all other people, and he gives us the hope that we will one day see both Jesus and our loved ones again.

Prayer: *Wonderful Counsellor, thank you for coming to live among us. Help us to show warmth to everyone we meet. Amen*

Thought for the day: How can I show Christ's compassion to everyone I meet?

Lauren Craft (Virginia, US)

Comfort and peace

Read 2 Corinthians 1:1–7

The peace of God, which surpasses all understanding, will guard your hearts and your minds in Christ Jesus.
Philippians 4:7 (NRSV)

Our congregation was shocked when our minister's wife, Susan, died unexpectedly at the age of 55. She had been taking care of her mother some miles away, so our minister immediately left to handle matters. I was asked on a Friday to lead the service on Sunday. I readily accepted, but I struggled with what I would say to our grieving congregation.

That Sunday morning, I went through my daily routine of reading *The Upper Room* and my Bible, then spending time in prayer. The devotion for the day was about finding peace in loss. The writer closed the devotion with a reference to Philippians 4:7 and God's promise of a peace that passes our understanding. I felt that God had arranged that devotion on that day to help me find the right message for the congregation.

During the service, I read the devotion aloud. In the days and weeks that followed, I saw our congregation respond as brothers and sisters in Christ, reaching out with love and comfort to help our minister and his family in their time of need.

Prayer: *Heavenly Father, thank you for providing comfort and peace to us during challenging times. Help us to do the same for others. Amen*

Thought for the day: How will I be open to God's message for me today?

John D. Bown (Minnesota, US)

God already knows

Read Matthew 6:25–33

Seek first [your heavenly Father's] kingdom and his righteousness, and all these things will be given to you as well.

Matthew 6:33 (NIV)

A woman whom I had supervised at work 35 years before was about to retire, and she asked me to say a few words on her behalf at her leaving party. I happily agreed. She mentioned how grateful she had been that I had spoken about her to the management of the company and had suggested that she should be promoted. I had not remembered anything about this incident. But when I realised the way God had used me to meet her needs, her retirement party turned out to be a blessing for me as well.

God is always with us, knows our needs and sends others to help us. Then we, in turn, can help others. We just have to trust that God will lead the way. Then, our job is to obey and follow him.

Prayer: *God, our guide, thank you for caring for our needs. Help us to seek first your kingdom and your righteousness as we receive your blessings and help others. Amen*

Thought for the day: God can bless me by giving me opportunities to serve others.

Joan A. Brathwaite (Christ Church, Barbados)

Unconventional places

Read Ephesians 2:1–10
We are God's handiwork, created in Christ Jesus to do good works, which God prepared in advance for us to do.
Ephesians 2:10 (NIV)

Strip clubs aren't places you would typically expect a church group to go in search of friends. But for years, my friend Tonya and other women from her church went there regularly to cultivate relationships. With permission from the club's owners, the church women gave female employees free toiletries. Many of the recipients were single mothers, struggling to make ends meet, and they gladly received the gifts. After a while, the church group found opportunities to meet with the women during non-work hours. They listened, offered support, met practical needs and shared spiritual truth about Jesus from the Bible.

It took courage and perseverance to do something so unconventional. Was it without risk? Definitely not. Was it Christlike? Absolutely.

Jesus invited all kinds of people to come into the kingdom of God. It didn't matter if onlookers misunderstood or gossiped. Everyone needs God's grace. If we're followers of Jesus, we'll look for ways to extend it – even in unconventional places.

Prayer: *God of all, open our eyes and hearts to the hurting world around us. Help us to take every opportunity to share our faith with others. In Jesus' name we pray. Amen*

Thought for the day: Where might I interact with someone who needs the gospel?

Terri Foster (South Carolina, US)

A single red feather

Read Psalm 91:1–6

Keep me as the apple of your eye; hide me in the shadow of your wings.

Psalm 17:8 (NIV)

As predicted, the severe thunderstorms had blown through our area with a vengeance; but now the sun shone more radiantly than usual. Yet I felt as broken as the tree limbs I was collecting. The weight of the world pressed on me: concerns over my family's health, money, fractured relationships. I struggled to banish these issues from my thoughts. I tried to focus on the blessings I had received and on those yet to come.

The joyful trill of birds filtered through my disturbed thoughts. As I listened, a blackbird landed on a branch directly above me. He threw back his head and serenaded me with gusto. His voice rose above all the other birds' songs. Enthralled, I watched him for several minutes until a single red feather fluttered in the breeze and landed at my feet. The feather was perfect, just as God had created it.

I saved the feather and laminated it in plastic for use as a bookmark. It now marks Psalm 91 in my Bible as a reminder of God's steadfast presence in my life. To me the feather represents hope. I know I cannot expect a trouble-free life. Regardless of the trials that come my way, I am assured that God is with me and that I will always find refuge beneath his sheltering wings.

Prayer: *Dear heavenly Father, thank you for being our shield and protection through the trials we face. Help us to see the joy in each day. Amen*

Thought for the day: Today, I will find joy in God's creation.

Jeanne C. Gore (North Carolina, US)

Just as I am

Read 2 Corinthians 12:6–11

[The Lord] said to me, 'My grace is sufficient for you, for my power is made perfect in weakness.'
2 Corinthians 12:9 (NIV)

Most of my religious friends seem to think that religious people should fit a particular mould. I am outgoing and inquisitive, and my friends don't think I should behave that way. I love spending time with other Christians, but I couldn't hide my true self to fit their idea of what I should be like. Many times I have been confronted and attacked based on my personality, and so I have come to think I should change, vigorously begging God to help me.

I waited for God to remove my extrovert tendencies so that I would appear 'spiritual' to my church and my religious friends. Then these words gave me perspective: God's 'grace is sufficient for me'. I now see that my outgoing personality gives me opportunities to initiate conversations. Knowing who I am in God has helped me to speak to others who feel rejected, for I know God is there with me. I have now more fully experienced love from God, the one who accepts me just as I am.

What an encouragement to know that the Lord can be glorified even when we are misunderstood and misjudged. We can come to God – just as we are.

Prayer: *Dear Saviour, thank you for loving us as we are. Help us to make our lives reflect the truth of your word. Amen*

Thought for the day: Even when I don't love myself, God loves me just as I am.

Timothy Olumide (Osun, Nigeria)

From despair to hope

Read Psalm 5

Let all who take refuge in you be glad; let them ever sing for joy.
Psalm 5:11 (NIV)

How are you today? Feeling good or feeling unwell or anxious? The news we hear on radio, on television, in newspapers or on social media isn't always uplifting. Personal news, too, may not be good and we may begin to despair.

Psalm 5, like many of the psalms, starts with despair and ends with hope: 'Listen to my words, Lord… Hear my cry for help,' and then 'Let all who take refuge in you be glad; let them ever sing for joy.'

Such rejoicing may appear simplistic in a world that seems to lurch uncontrollably through suffering, weariness and fear. David the psalmist would empathise. In the space of a few roller-coaster lines he expresses dismay and disenchantment before turning to trust and confidence in God.

Tension, testing and turbulence strike everyone – you, me, Jesus himself. But the Prince of Peace has conquered evil, and one day all will be well. So we can be glad because God is trustworthy in his loving and saving power. Not a case of 'We will overcome', but 'He has overcome.'

Prayer: *Lord God, you hold the whole world in your hands. Help us to trust you through testing times as well as good times. Amen*

Thought for the day: I will keep my eyes fixed on Jesus and be glad.

Pam Pointer (Wiltshire, United Kingdom)

Sleep in peace

Read Psalm 121
Trust in the Lord with all your heart.
Proverbs 3:5 (NRSV)

One night when my younger brother and I were children, he had a nightmare. I gave him a hug and told him to go back to sleep. But he said the nightmare kept coming back every time he closed his eyes. So I suggested that he talk to God. He sat down, prayed and then slept in peace. He didn't even need a hug from me anymore!

I am still amazed at the sincerity of a little child's heart – the ability to simply trust God. When my brother ended his prayer, he truly believed that God had listened to him and would guard him through the night.

As an adult, I have often recalled that moment when I faced fear and uncertainty. At those times, I remind myself to trust God with all my heart and to worry less – to believe that he watches over me in every situation. I have learned to let God take over what I cannot control. When I do, he grants me peace.

Prayer: *Dear God, help us to have a heart like a little child, to trust that you will show us the way through any fearful situation. We pray as Jesus taught us, 'Our Father which art in heaven, Hallowed be thy name. Thy kingdom come. Thy will be done, as in heaven, so in earth. Give us day by day our daily bread. And forgive us our sins; for we also forgive every one that is indebted to us. And lead us not into temptation; but deliver us from evil.'* Amen*

Thought for the day: Today I will worry less and trust God more.

Juita Kartini (Jakarta Raya, Indonesia)

PRAYER FOCUS: CHILDREN SUFFERING FROM NIGHTMARES
*Luke 11:2–4 (KJV)

A Christian legacy

Read Romans 12:9–21

What does the Lord require of you? To act justly and to love mercy and to walk humbly with your God.
Micah 6:8 (NIV)

One day while cooking yet another big meal in our family kitchen, I sighed and asked aloud, 'What will others remember most about me when I'm gone? The cooking or the cleaning?' My husband jokingly suggested this inscription for my future tombstone: 'She made good bread.'

This humorous exchange led me to do some serious thinking about the legacy I will leave. In Western culture, corporations, churches, families and even individuals are often charged with composing a mission statement, a reason for doing what they do. An even more daring challenge is to encourage individuals to write their obituary while they are still able to do so. If we think ahead about what we want said about us at the end of our life, we will be motivated to live up to those words.

I know that the best words for me to live up to are found in today's reading, which I carry around in my purse. These verses guide my daily life. They tell me how to love others and when. As followers of Christ, we can find our life's mission statement powerfully stated in these words.

Prayer: *Our loving Father, we pray that the world will see Christ in us more every day and come to know your grace and loving-kindness through us – all to your glory. Amen*

Thought for the day: What do I want my legacy as a follower of Christ to be?

Wilma Rose Vernich (Tennessee, US)

A lesson in forgiveness

Read James 1:19–25

If you forgive the sins of any, they are forgiven them; if you retain the sins of any, they are retained.
John 20:23 (NRSV)

Years ago, I taught a Sunday school class. One Sunday, after a particularly trying week, I walked into the room at church to find paper streamers hanging from the light fixtures, chairs on the tables and the children grinning at me.

I began to scold them angrily for their disregard for me and church property. I went on for a while, ignoring their hurt looks, before I realised what I was doing. Then I stopped and apologised. I explained that my wife was seriously ill in hospital, and I was so worried that I wasn't thinking straight – but that was no reason to treat them so badly.

We then went on with our Sunday school lesson. At the end, I stood at the door to watch them leave. I was proud of the example of forgiveness I had shown them. As they left, each member of the class gave me a hug or a pat on the shoulder. I was happy that they had learned their lesson on forgiveness. But as I thought about it later, I realised that they were the teachers and I was the pupil. They had each freely expressed their forgiveness for my unfair rant; as they left the classroom talking and laughing, they made no reference to what had happened. That kind of forgiveness is a true gift from God.

Prayer: *Dear Lord, thank you for the gift of forgiveness. Help us to forgive as completely as those young believers. Amen*

Thought for the day: How do I express my complete forgiveness of others?

Ken Claar (Idaho, US)

'When you're smiling'

Read Numbers 6:22–27

The Lord make his face shine on you and be gracious to you.
Numbers 6:25 (NIV)

From 4.00 to 6.00 each morning I spend time in prayer and devotion. I find it is the best time to talk to God, praising and thanking him for each new day. As I was meditating one morning, I thought: 'What does God's smile look like? What can we do to make God smile?' Just then, the young man who delivers the newspaper called at my door. Every morning when he greets me with a warm smile, I imagine God smiling upon me.

A smile can bring encouragement to someone who is sad or lonely, a way of saying to someone who is heartbroken, 'Wait on the Lord. God loves you and so do I.' A good deed paired with a smile can assist the vulnerable, the aged or children without parents. It can give support to the local shopkeepers in my community. A passing smile to those we encounter might be just enough to offer hope.

What does God's smile look like? It looks like the smile we give to all those around us. It looks like the joy we bring to others in our words and deeds. When I return a smile, I know that God is smiling upon me as well.

Prayer: *God of joy and blessing, thank you for your smile that we see reflected each day on the faces of all who believe in you. Amen*

Thought for the day: When I smile at others – via words or deeds – God smiles at me.

Laura Cristina Quintana de Mota (Dominican Republic)

Sharing prayer

Read Ephesians 6:12–18

Pray in the Spirit on all occasions with all kinds of prayers and requests. With this in mind, be alert and always keep on praying for all the Lord's people.

Ephesians 6:18 (NIV)

Late one evening, my husband became very ill and started bleeding. We rushed him to hospital, and after a very long wait he was finally admitted for further treatment. On my way home, I found myself waiting in a traffic queue where the police were checking vehicles. As the line progressed, I wondered, 'Why tonight? Why now?'

When it was my turn, the police officer asked where I was going. I replied, 'I'm going home. I've just come from the hospital.' Hearing that, his demeanour changed, and he asked if everything was all right. I replied, 'I hope so.' Then he asked if he could pray for me. I immediately agreed, and he offered up a wonderful prayer. He didn't know the circumstances, but his words were just what I needed to hear. At that moment, we found ourselves linked together as two disciples sharing God's love.

The next morning, my husband was discharged from the hospital. His health problems that followed were difficult, but we knew that we were in God's loving hands.

Prayer: *Dear Father, thank you for the honour of praying for others. Help us to be aware of the needs of those around us. Amen*

Thought for the day: Every day I will open my eyes and spirit to opportunities to pray for others.

Connie Downs (California, US)

Coming near to God

Read 1 Corinthians 9:24–27

Come near to God and he will come near to you.
James 4:8 (NIV)

I clutched my side and felt a pulsing sensation in my throat. With each laboured breath, my chest heaved up and down. I had finished my first 5K run, just before my 51st birthday.

I had started running just one year earlier. In those early days, I jogged only when I felt like it and at a speed that felt comfortable. My approach did not yield great results. Then I discovered a plan.

My strategy began with walking for a few minutes, followed by running for 60 seconds. The alternating walking/jogging schedule increased until after a couple of weeks I could run five minutes non-stop. Instead of feeling exhausted with limbs too heavy to move, I felt refreshed.

Distance running required disciplining my physical life. Likewise, we strengthen our spiritual lives through the disciplines of Bible study, meditation, fasting and prayer. A Bible-reading plan and a designated time and place of prayer help me stay focused as I come near to God. Coming close to God requires directing our hearts towards him – not with a prescribed list of activities to earn his favour but rather an out-pouring of desire to spend time with him. And just as today's verse promises, God comes near to us.

Prayer: *O Lord, increase our desire to know you better. Amen*

Thought for the day: I come close to God by spending time with him.

Barbara Gordon (Missouri, US)

PRAYER FOCUS: THOSE BEGINNING A NEW SPIRITUAL DISCIPLINE

Genuine support

Read 2 Corinthians 9:6–11

They all ate and were satisfied, and the disciples picked up twelve basketfuls of broken pieces that were left over.
Matthew 14:20 (NIV)

I retired a long time ago, but I have not been able to fulfil my desire to go abroad as a volunteer evangelist. In the meantime, I have chosen to support others in this work. Recently I heard from a missionary who was desperate because the church that had supplied his major funding could no longer support him. In vain, I begged several other churches to help him.

One morning while praying, I remembered the story of Jesus' feeding the five thousand. When the disciples suggested that he send the crowds away, Jesus replied, 'They do not need to go away; you give them something to eat' (Matthew 14:16). Five loaves of bread and two fish were inadequate to feed 5,000 people just as the rod in Moses' hand could not free the Israelites from Egypt. But in both cases, God supplied what the people needed. Yet I had nothing that would help this missionary. Still, this passage remained with me. Then I remembered a small savings account that I had put aside years before for emergency use.

I have decided I will no longer beg money from other people or organisations for this missionary but instead will give him what I have. Just as God gave manna and quail to the Israelites in the desert (see Exodus 16), I believe that when we are willing to give to others, God will provide for us.

Prayer: *God of all grace, remind us that we always have something that we can give to those in need. Amen*

Thought for the day: My willingness to serve may be an answer to prayer.

Seung Jae Oh (Chungnam, South Korea)

God's promises

Read Isaiah 45:2–6

I will go before thee, and make the crooked places straight.
Isaiah 45:2 (KJV)

When I was a young girl, my mother gave me a small box of cards containing God's promises from scripture. Each morning before school, we selected one to read. Those promises stayed with us all day and were a comfort when challenges arose. This tradition carried over into my marriage, motherhood and divorce.

Years later, a major crisis hit my family when my adult daughter fell down some stairs and suffered a traumatic brain injury. Brain surgery followed. I was told that if she survived, the recovery process would take months or years of rehab and that the prognosis for total recovery was doubtful.

Machines pumped oxygen, fluids and food into her body. I was at first terrified, then angry. 'Why us?' I thought. During another sleepless night, I sat up in bed and began to pray. I asked God to direct me. When I had finished, I glanced over to the chest of drawers and spotted my box of scripture promises. 'Guide my hand, dear Lord,' I whispered, as I drew out a card. It read, 'We know that all things work together for good for those who love God' (Romans 8:28, NRSV). Immediately, God's peace began to replace my anguish. How marvellous to have the promises of a living, loving God, who guides us and gives us comfort during life's challenges!

Prayer: *Thank you, God, for your constant help, guidance and healing power. Help us always to trust you. Amen*

Thought for the day: I will keep God's promises close.

Arlene Rains Graber (Kansas, US)

A new beginning

Read Genesis 50:15–21

If anyone is in Christ, there is a new creation: everything old has passed away; see, everything has become new!
2 Corinthians 5:17 (NRSV)

I was born in Ryazan, Russia, in 1999. My parents were alcoholics who took me to bars when I was very young. A few days after my third birthday they lost their rights to keep me, and I was placed in an orphanage. The orphanage was full – about 40 children, including my brother. I was too young at the time to understand what was happening. When I was four, an American couple adopted me and brought me to Fort Worth, Texas, where my new life began. I grew up with three American sisters and my brother, Kole, who was also adopted from Russia. My parents put me in a good school where I received an amazing education, which eventually brought me to college where I plan to study business management.

When I was in that orphanage, I had no clue what my life was going to look like. But God knew. He sent loving parents to adopt me and bring me up to be the best person I can be. I do not know what my future holds, but I know it will be used to glorify God's kingdom.

Prayer: *Dear Lord, thank you for turning our night into day, redeeming us and giving us second chances. Amen*

Thought for the day: I know that my future is in God's hands.

Alex Jordan (Texas, US)

Pruning

Read Hebrews 12:4–11

No discipline seems pleasant at the time, but painful. Later on, however, it produces a harvest of righteousness and peace for those who have been trained by it.

Hebrews 12:11 (NIV)

I was going through a rough patch in my relationship with someone very dear to me. I felt that I had done nothing to deserve the painful words and attitudes. Angry and resentful, I knew that I could either shut this person out or lean on God. I chose to lean on God.

As I prayed, cried and read my Bible, I experienced God's comfort. I was reassured of God's deep love for me and reminded to find my worth in him (see 1 John 3:1). But something else was at work in me that I wasn't prepared for. God gently helped me to see my wrong attitudes and actions towards the person who had hurt me and showed me how that had caused some of their behaviour. I felt God was using this experience to prune me.

At first I was annoyed. How had someone's wrong treatment of me turned into a conviction for my soul? It didn't seem fair. Then I remembered what pruning does: it cuts away what is harmful, unnecessary or growth-inhibiting. The result is healthy growth and bountiful fruit. Instead of resenting this person, I decided to be grateful that my loving God was 'cutting me back' so that I could spring forward with new growth and healthier relationships.

Prayer: *Dear God, give us the peace to accept pruning from your loving hands. Amen*

Thought for the day: How is God pruning me?

Esther MacDonald (Quebec, Canada)

Smallest acts

Read Luke 7:36–50

As [a woman who lived a sinful life] stood behind [Jesus] at his feet weeping, she began to wet his feet with her tears. Then she wiped them with her hair, kissed them and poured perfume on them.
Luke 7:38 (NIV)

Shortly before I retired from 40 years of teaching physical education, a young student gave me a red pipe cleaner, roughly shaped like a heart. I attached it to my bookcase as a reminder of his thoughtfulness. Several years later, it's still there. Whenever I look at that irregularly shaped heart, I smile.

Sometimes I wonder if God looks at our offerings of love that way. God – the source and giver of all love – could perfectly do anything that we do for him. But I suspect that he delights in even our smallest acts of love.

Throughout scripture, Jesus commends any display of love for him. Jesus praised Mary's devotion as she listened attentively at his feet (see Luke 10:38–42). Upon spotting Zacchaeus' determination to see him, Jesus asked to share a meal with him (see Luke 19:1–10). Jesus affirmed the love of the woman who kissed and anointed his feet. Jesus accepted love, no matter how it was shown.

Whether we give our love by praising God, stopping to admire creation or helping someone in need, we can offer everything to him, and graciously respond to those who show us love in big or small ways.

Prayer: *Dear Lord, thank you for showing us how to love others. Help us to share your love with the world. Amen*

Thought for the day: God teaches me how to give and receive love.

Lin Daniels (Massachusetts, US)

Hopes and aspirations

Read Hebrews 6:17–20

I press on to take hold of that for which Christ Jesus took hold of me.
Philippians 3:12 (NIV)

Someone asked a barefoot child, 'What will you be when you grow up?' 'I want to be President,' he replied with confidence. A little girl who lived on the streets said she intended to be a doctor to help her people. The hopes and aspirations of childhood! We must have hopes, but they can fade with the years. Many people, disillusioned, turn to drugs or other destructive habits; some are tempted to suicide. Do they feel there is nothing to aspire to?

I was a disillusioned teenager until I learned that God was holding out to me a hope of real, eternal life. And all I had to do was to take hold of him! Our reading shows that this God-given hope is 'an anchor for the soul, firm and secure'.

Paul knew that there was yet more for him to take hold of. Jesus had given him a goal – to fulfil the whole calling of God for his life. With a secure anchor, I can aspire to all that God wants to do in and through me.

Prayer: *Lord, I know that I am secure in my hold on you. Help me to move forward into all that you have prepared for me to be and do. Amen*

Thought for the day: I will hold on to my hope in God.

Marion Turnbull (Merseyside, United Kingdom)

Taste and see

Read Psalm 34:1–8

O taste and see that the Lord is good; happy are those who take refuge in him.

Psalm 34:8 (NRSV)

The pungent smell of the durian fruit brings back fond childhood memories for me. My late father used to lug home sacks of durians from Malaysia, and my family of six would gather round the table to enjoy this delicacy. It was an important family time for me.

In the past, it seemed a long wait until the durian season, when we could once again enjoy the fruit. These days, durians are readily available in many places, even in supermarkets. Most people just take them for granted.

Those who have never tasted the durian may simply be put off by its unpleasant smell and its thorny appearance. Likewise, those who do not know Jesus Christ, the king of kings, or have never tasted his goodness, may just turn away from him, based on limited understanding of who he is. But by opening our hearts to God's goodness revealed in Jesus we can find the joy that comes when we make a commitment to follow him, wherever he may lead us.

Prayer: *Dear Lord Jesus, thank you for your love and the gift of salvation. Help us to discover your goodness as we learn to trust in you. Amen*

Thought for the day: When I take a step of faith to follow Jesus, I will surely taste God's goodness.

Florence Fong (Singapore)

Walking by faith

Read John 20:24–31

Jesus told [Thomas], 'Because you have seen me, you have believed; blessed are those who have not seen and yet have believed.'
John 20:29 (NIV)

Our new house in a different part of the country is close to a small wooded ravine. One day after work, my wife asked me if I had heard the owl that morning.

'I don't think owls live in this area,' I replied. 'Are you sure it was an owl?' Although sceptical, I was willing to acknowledge that maybe owls sound different here. Two weeks later, early on a Saturday morning while sitting at the breakfast table, I heard the familiar hoot of an owl. And then a week later my wife reported seeing an owl fly about two feet from the windscreen of her car. This time I believed her. She had seen the owl face to face, and I had heard it. I became an owl believer!

For many years I was an agnostic. I wanted more proof. I wanted to hear Jesus' voice, see him face to face or, like Thomas, to put my hand into his side. Yet after seeing the love of others who called themselves Christians and hearing the voice of the Saviour through scripture, I became a believer. In this age, we walk by faith, without physical proof. Yet we do have the promise that if we will seek, we will find (see Deuteronomy 4:29; Matthew 7:7; Luke 11:9). And someday – some glorious day – we will see Jesus Christ face to face.

Prayer: *Dear God, help us to be lights to show others how to see and hear the truth of our Saviour. In Jesus' name we pray. Amen*

Thought for the day: How can I help others to hear the voice of God?

Mike C. Bertoglio (Georgia, US)

Love is…

Read 1 Corinthians 13:4–7

Be completely humble and gentle; be patient, bearing with one another in love.
Ephesians 4:2 (NIV)

Walking down the pavement towards the old, two-storey school building, I heard the happy voices of pupils in the courtyard. A new school year was beginning with its many new experiences and opportunities for learning. Some of the pupils I would be teaching had not yet fully mastered the English language, and others had learning difficulties. Many challenges lay ahead.

As part of my morning devotions, I had read what is sometimes called 'the love chapter' – 1 Corinthians 13. A Sunday school teacher once explained verses 4–7 of chapter 13 by suggesting that in place of the words 'love' and 'it' we substitute the word 'Jesus' and read through the verses again. Because we seek to be like Jesus and show his love, she then asked us to replace the words 'love' and 'it' with our name and read the verses through a third time. In doing so, each of us was reminded of the type of love that God shows us. That is the type of love that God wants me to share with my pupils and everyone around me each day.

Prayer: *Loving God, help us to show love, patience and kindness to everyone we meet. Amen*

Thought for the day: How can I show kindness and the love of God to others today?

Pam Hickerson (Texas, US)

God's peace

Read Psalm 120

I'm for peace, but when I speak, they are for war.
Psalm 120:7 (CEB)

In Psalm 120, it seems that the psalmist was getting frustrated at not finding any peace at all in his surroundings – or even the entire world. In a state of great stress and agony, he was asking God to deliver him from the corrupt minds who do not accept peace.

In today's world, we also may feel devastated because we cannot find peace. At times it seems that some people do not want peace, and as a result peace feels impossible to achieve. The stress of constant war and conflict makes us tired and discouraged. We see some people fighting for selfish interests, some for what they believe in and some against ideas they oppose.

The glory of God's peace is not in winning; it is about living in God's way – following the prince of peace, who told his disciples, 'Peace I leave with you; my peace I give you. I do not give to you as the world gives. Do not let your hearts be troubled and do not be afraid' (John 14:27, NIV).

Prayer: *God of peace, comfort those who are living in great turmoil, and rescue those who face persecution. Grant them your peace. In the name of Jesus, we pray. Amen*

Thought for the day: Even in countries torn by war, I can find God's peace.

Aftab Yunis Hakim (Punjab, Pakistan)

An act of compassion

Read Colossians 3:12–17

In humility value others above yourselves, not looking to your own interests but each of you to the interests of the others.
Philippians 2:3–4 (NIV)

Seventeen years ago, my son was sentenced to life in prison. It was a time full of grief for many reasons and for so many people. As the courtroom emptied after the sentencing, a man approached me. I recognised him as the one who had carried his Bible to court every day – the victim's father. Standing quietly, looking into his face and not knowing what to expect, I was surprised when suddenly he said to me, 'I am sorry for your loss.' In the midst of the most devastating event in my life, God had placed before me this gentleman – in mourning himself – to express his compassion and sorrow.

This man had shown me the kindest act of Christian compassion that I have ever witnessed. In one brief moment, through him, God took my grief away and showed me a picture of the compassion and love of a true follower of our Saviour Jesus Christ.

Prayer: *Compassionate God, thank you for the people who show others your blessings, mercy and grace. Amen*

Thought for the day: I will give thanks to God for teaching me through others.

Lisa Scallio (Maryland, US)

Keep singing!

Read Psalm 104:31–34

Teach and admonish one another in all wisdom; and with gratitude in your hearts sing psalms, hymns, and spiritual songs to God.
Colossians 3:16 (NRSV)

When my wife and I moved into a care home, our minds were alert and active, but our bodies were less than strong. As we settled in, I realised that my ability to think, converse and lead others was well ahead of many of the other residents. In talking with them, I learned that many were experiencing sadness, even depression. So I thought I would offer encouragement, even in small ways.

I decided to lead an occasional singsong after dinner. The first night, more than 30 people came! I used a songbook I had saved from my school days and made copies of the songs' words for everyone. A young man who was an excellent pianist came to accompany us. Through the songs I chose I tried to reveal the presence of God's Spirit. It worked! The response was positive, so I decided to keep on singing with them. Singing can lift our spirits and point us towards God.

Prayer: *O God, keep us singing so that we sense your Holy Spirit bringing us encouragement and hope. Amen*

Thought for the day: The gift of song can draw me close to God and others.

Ron L. Keller (Michigan, US)

Laying aside every weight

Read Hebrews 12:1–3

Let us also lay aside every weight and the sin that clings so closely, and let us run with perseverance the race that is set before us, looking to Jesus the pioneer and perfecter of our faith.
Hebrews 12:1–2 (NRSV)

One morning as I prepared for work, I was trying to decide what to carry in my handbag and what to leave behind. The issue was not the handbag's capacity but its weight. I wondered how many people would see me struggling with my handbag and not understand why I was dragging my feet early in the morning. Another part of me thought that I could hide my struggle and carry the full bag, but it would eventually tire me.

We have many weights to carry – family identity, our jobs and other responsibilities – and we have to carry them all in one body. It might not show at first as we go through our days, but eventually we will grow weary. The verse above reminds us that we can run with perseverance as we lay aside every weight and look to Jesus, the pioneer and perfecter of our faith. We can rely on him to help us face every challenge before us. We don't have to do it alone.

Prayer: *Dear Lord Jesus, thank you for giving us rest as we lay aside every weight in our lives. In Jesus' name. Amen*

Thought for the day: No burden is too heavy as long as I am with Jesus.

Vimbai Chizarura (Harare, Zimbabwe)

The delight of prayer

Read John 17:1–8

It is God who establishes us with you in Christ and has anointed us, by putting his seal on us and giving us his Spirit in our hearts as a first instalment.

2 Corinthians 1:21–22 (NRSV)

As a part of a prayer chain at our church, I delighted in the opportunity to pray for others. I was able to grow spiritually and offer God's love to others.

Whenever I received a call, I would immediately step into my quiet space with Bible in hand. The Lord would direct me to an appropriate scripture. Then I prayed the scripture for the person requesting prayer. I did not have to know any details. I did not have to learn the results. My task was to lift the person through God's word, God's promise.

When we moved to a new town, I lost my connection with the prayer chain. But the Lord gave me a new source for knowing whom to pray for. Now my friends request prayer through social media, sometimes for themselves and sometimes for loved ones.

Through this experience, I am learning how to pray more effectively in my daily quiet time. I can listen for the nudge of appropriate scripture in any situation, pray that scripture and then leave all in the loving hands of our Lord. What a delight!

Prayer: *Thank you, loving God, for giving us the opportunity to pray for others. We know you hear and answer each prayer. In Christ's name. Amen*

Thought for the day: For whom can I pray today?

Dusty Reed (Iowa, US)

An ever-present help

Read Psalm 46:1–11

God is our refuge and strength.
Psalm 46:1 (NIV)

My part of the country has experienced many destructive storms this summer. They often bring with them huge hailstones that can crash through car windscreens, destroy crops and even kill our livestock. The psalmist, seeking to bring courage and hope to God's suffering people, wrote about such destruction.

As we read the verses of Psalm 46, we can be comforted through the many storms we have experienced. When we see houses damaged and businesses ruined by the weather, we begin to realise how vulnerable we are. So we turn to God for strength in the midst of our weakness and fear.

When we turn to God in the face of storms of any kind, we can find our faith deepened and we realise that we are not alone. God, 'our refuge and strength, an ever-present help in trouble', is the one who causes fear to dissipate and gives us courage to forge ahead through every adversity we may face.

Prayer: *God of eternity, open our eyes to see that you are nearer than we can imagine, closer than a friend or brother. Amen*

Thought for the day: Even when I feel alone, God is with me.

Al Trucano* (Nebraska, US)

*The author passed away before the publication of this issue.

Restored

Read Job 37:14–24

God's voice thunders in marvellous ways; he does great things beyond our understanding.
Job 37:5 (NIV)

When I became ill and my business failed, I was abandoned by the people who were close to me. Some people thought that I must have committed a great sin and was being punished for it. Some people advised me to seek healing from another god. I lost hope and complained to God, 'Why should I experience all these things? Why did you not immediately lift me up and restore my business?'

In the silence, God spoke to me through Elihu's words in Job 37. After tragedies befell Job, most of Job's friends came with a variety of advice and opinions. But Elihu talked about God's power.

These verses reminded me that we can see God's power and glory in the universe through creation. God's wisdom is unfathomable, and he does great things beyond our understanding. He restored Job and blessed the latter part of Job's life more than the former part (see Job 42:12). The story of Job helped me to continue to trust in God despite my hardships. God restored me and blessed me, as he wants to restore and bless all of us.

Prayer: *Dear God, teach us to see your glory and to give thanks for your faithful love and care. Amen*

Thought for the day: I can see God's power and glory through creation.

Linda Chandra (Banten, Indonesia)

People of peace

Read 2 Corinthians 5:17–21

We are… Christ's ambassadors, as though God were making his appeal through us.
2 Corinthians 5:20 (NIV)

Last autumn, my autistic son was struggling at school with an impatient, inexperienced teacher. After daily unpleasant encounters, he became anxious and began to lose his love for learning. As his main carer, I attempted to communicate with the teacher for several months, only to be ignored.

Later, as I was reading 2 Corinthians 5, God reminded me that I had been called to be a person of peace. I had become more focused on injustice than love, more intent on being right than seeking resolution. When I repented, God showed me that underneath the teacher's prickly, defensive reactions was a person leading a challenging class and having constantly to prove herself to keep her job. My heart was moved from irritation and outrage to compassion and understanding. I began to pray for this teacher daily, and God empowered me to respond to her with words of encouragement and peace. Over time, the teacher changed her approach, treating my son with greater patience, gentleness and consideration for his challenges.

God asks us to be Christ's representatives to those around us. When others are angry, defensive or hurt, we are called to respond as God does to us: with compassion, love and peace. Through our prayers and Christlike responses, God's transforming love can heal the hearts of those around us and bring peace to all of us.

Prayer: *Dear God, thank you for helping us to respond in love to everyone we encounter today. Amen*

Thought for the day: Today I will show God's love by responding peacefully.

Sara Hague (Oregon, US)

Our gifts and our service

Read Philippians 2:1–4

Each of you should use whatever gift you have received to serve others, as faithful stewards of God's grace in its various forms.
1 Peter 4:10 (NIV)

When I had finished the sermon, I prepared to celebrate Holy Communion. I asked Lina to help me in serving the elements. After the service, Lina's mother cried with joy. Lina is deaf and communicates using sign language. Her mother recalled how she endured distress because of her daughter's condition. But when she saw her assisting during Holy Communion, she understood that Lina communicates with God in a unique way and does it joyfully.

A faithful Christian, Lina is independent, caring and valued in the church and where she works. She is filled with God's love and grace as she communicates through sign language to others who are deaf. Instead of being constrained by what she cannot do, Lina abides in the hope of one day being involved in formal ministry wherever God can use her gifts and her service.

God delights in the variety of ways we serve others and share the love of Christ with the world.

Prayer: *God of grace, grant us the wisdom to acknowledge and honour the gifts of all your people who seek to serve you with a joyful heart in unique and wonderful ways. We pray in the name of Jesus. Amen*

Thought for the day: God rejoices in all our differing abilities.

Juan Guerrero (Colombia)

God's help

Read Hebrews 4:12–16

Let us then approach God's throne of grace with confidence, so that we may receive mercy and find grace to help us in our time of need.
Hebrews 4:16 (NIV)

Everything went wrong that week. Three managers usually ran the residential care floor, but one was on maternity leave and another needed emergency heart surgery.

Still, I managed all the resident and employee issues. But when two staff members called in sick, I was frantic to find enough staff. When the third employee called in sick, I broke down in tears and cried out, 'I can't do this anymore!' A colleague heard me crying and stopped to help. We talked, I cried and she helped me piece a plan together.

When I became overwhelmed, I was blind to any solution to my problem. Yet I thought I should handle it myself instead of asking for assistance. In the same way, we sometimes don't ask for the Lord's help until we're overwhelmed with our burdens and fears. We forget that we don't have to handle life on our own.

I realised that I should have asked for God's guidance. After that, I began praying for God's wisdom each day. As I did so, I found I was less stressed when things didn't go as planned. I learned that I don't have to cry to get God's attention either — he hears even a whispered, 'Help me, Father.'

Prayer: *Thank you, Lord, for the availability of your help. Remind us to rely on your power instead of our own. Amen*

Thought for the day: God's help is available to me when I ask.

Diana L. Walters (Tennessee, US)

Two brothers

Read Luke 15:1–3, 11–32

We had to celebrate and rejoice, because this brother of yours was dead and has come to life; he was lost and has been found.
Luke 15:32 (NRSV)

As the elder of two brothers, I have always felt that the elder brother in the story of the prodigal son has been treated unfairly. To me, his objections are justified. I am sure that this feeling was due in part to the similarities between their story and my relationship with my brother. I was always the responsible, dutiful stay-at-home child. He was the spendthrift, wandering from home and spending time in questionable company. I once gave him my old car because I felt sorry for him; he sold it and used the money for things I don't want to know about.

But just as in the parable, my brother eventually came to himself and returned home – literally and figuratively. He has been a recovering alcoholic for over a decade and has mentored many other recovering alcoholics.

Jesus' parable is about how to love unconditionally. God does not reject us for reckless living or for unforgiving hearts. He loves both the prodigal and the self-righteous. We are not told how the elder brother responded to his father's plea for love. But we are invited to ponder how we would respond.

Prayer: *God of mercy, when we have wandered away from your presence, call us back. In Christ's name we pray. Amen*

Thought for the day: Whether I am reckless or self-righteous, God loves me.

Michael A. Macdonald (North Carolina, US)

Waiting

Read Isaiah 40:28–31

They that wait upon the Lord shall renew their strength.
Isaiah 40:31 (KJV)

I hate waiting. For me waiting is wasting time. I want the plane to take off once I am seated. I expect the waiter to bring the food soon after I place my order at a restaurant. Waiting makes me feel angry, frustrated and even hopeless.

When my home was damaged by Hurricane Irma, my nephew said he would do the repairs. But after I had waited two weeks, he still had not begun. Having little damage to my home, I had thought my repairs would be done quickly. But that was not the case; I had to wait. But as I waited, I learned that through the prophet Isaiah the Lord tells us that waiting can be a good thing. The prophet says, 'They that wait upon the Lord shall renew their strength.'

Shifting my attitude from one of 'impatiently waiting' to one of 'waiting upon the Lord' has taught me that God is working while I am waiting. This perspective has opened my eyes to the many gifts my heavenly Father has given me since I learned to wait. These gifts include renewed strength and purpose for my life.

God works to a different timetable from ours. If we are open as we wait, God can bless and shape us into the people he wants us to be.

Prayer: *Father God, teach us to wait upon you. Help us to know that you are always working for our good. Amen*

Thought for the day: When I wait on the Lord, I am not wasting time.

Berthille Laveist-Chittick (Sint Maarten, Netherlands)

Still the same inside

Read Matthew 19:13–15

Humans see only what is visible to the eyes, but the Lord sees into the heart.
1 Samuel 16:7 (CEB)

When our grandsons were aged four and six, my husband underwent chemotherapy. We wondered how the outward changes in him would affect them. After a momentary look of concern, four-year-old Seth went running to his grandpa and began to play as usual. Six-year-old Elliot said, 'It's okay, Grandpa, because you're still the same inside.' From then on, they seemed oblivious to the outward changes. They simply basked in the love of the man they knew to be kind and caring.

Many changes can cause us to appear different to one another: illness, aging, genetics, choices in clothing, hairstyles, etc. If we form opinions about one another based only upon outward appearances, we may miss opportunities to perceive the beauty of a 'gentle and quiet spirit' – the kind that is of 'great worth in God's sight' (1 Peter 3:4, NIV).

How blessed we are that God looks upon our hearts! When we seek to value what is in the hearts of others, our hearts will be pleasing to him.

Prayer: *Dear Father, help us to look beyond our differences and to seek your image within one another. Amen*

Thought for the day: I will value others the way God values me.

Sandra Sullivan (West Virginia, US)

Breathe, pray, believe

Read Psalm 40:1–10

*[The Lord] lifted me out of the slimy pit, out of the mud and mire;
he set my feet on a rock and gave me a firm place to stand.*
Psalm 40:2 (NIV)

I was 89 years old when illness and depression forced me to enter a nursing home for a time. There I faced the combined challenges of physical, emotional, spiritual and mental exhaustion. As I was so heavily dependent on others, it caused me to wonder if my lifetime of ministry as a pastor, chaplain and counsellor would help me now. During that frightening journey I found that my years of practising what I had taught others sustained me without my having to think about it. With great thanksgiving, I celebrated my 90th birthday with many friends in my own home.

On the day I was preparing to return home, a staff member said, 'When you came in here you were so ill. Now look at you! You're going home. What part did prayer and faith have in your healing?'

The question made me realise that prayer and faith are not new, additional or spectacular emergency items that we use during crises. Physical breathing, spiritual believing and praying without ceasing are ongoing practices essential to spiritual health. They sustain us not just in times of crisis but every day.

Prayer: *Kind-hearted Jesus, make us aware of your presence in every circumstance. Amen*

Thought for the day: God is as near as my latest breath.

Jack Albright (Kansas, US)

Detours

Read James 4:13–17

Many are the plans in a person's heart, but it is the Lord's purpose that prevails.
Proverbs 19:21 (NIV)

My sister-in-law and I had great plans for our holiday, and we had travelled hundreds of miles to our destination. We were going to have lots of early morning walks, enjoying the scenery. We were going to dip our toes in the ocean and breathe in the salty sea air. We also planned to tour a beautiful nature reserve and see the swans there.

That was all cut short when, five minutes after we arrived, my sister-in-law tripped over a step coming out of the house and injured her knee. Instead of long walks, we spent long hours at the hospital. Our plans had to change. Instead of morning walks, we had morning talks in the garden. Instead of exploring the nature reserve, we explored each other's lives and grew closer as we sat and chatted. This was a major detour from what we had planned, but it became a precious time together.

We are often disappointed or frustrated when things don't go according to our plans, but I have learned in these times to trust that God will use them for good. And without fail, each detour has drawn me closer to God and often helped me grow in mind and spirit. Thankfully, every change in direction comes with an unchanging God who guides us through it.

Prayer: *Dear God, help us to trust you no matter where life takes us. Give us peace in the midst of change. Amen*

Thought for the day: I will trust God in the midst of unexpected changes.

Linda Fasking (Kentucky, US)

An open invitation

Read Luke 14:15–24

Blessed is the one who will eat at the feast in the kingdom of God.
Luke 14:15 (NIV)

While I was in India staying with a woman named Nalini, a man named Kumar called round to help us organise a music workshop. Nalini invited him to stay for lunch. He declined graciously but did not leave. So she set a place for him, and he joined us at the table for a meal prepared by Nalini's daughter-in-law.

Kumar said, 'Since my wife left me years ago, I've been eating out in restaurants. Each has its own taste, but nothing as good as this. Whenever I'm asked to eat in someone's home, I always say no. But inwardly I'm longing for home-cooked meals.' Nalini's daughter-in-law replied, 'You must come often, Uncle.' I marvelled at her sincere, loving invitation to this man she had just met.

Jesus reminds us of the importance of warm invitations. He told the parable of a man who invited many guests to his feast in Luke 14. And in Matthew 11:28, Jesus says, 'Come to me, all you who are weary and burdened, and I will give you rest' (NIV). A joyous welcome awaits whoever comes to Jesus. Why hesitate? Jesus loves all people to the utmost and longs for us to enter a life-transforming relationship with him.

Prayer: *Lord Jesus, thank you for inviting us to your table. We come to you just as we are, asking you to live and reign in us. Amen*

Thought for the day: With whom can I share Christ's love today?

Lynda Samuel (Scotland, United Kingdom)

Unshakable

Read Romans 8:31–39

Neither death, nor life, nor angels, nor principalities, nor powers, nor things present, nor things to come… shall be able to separate us from the love of God, which is in Christ Jesus our Lord.
Romans 8:38–39 (KJV)

Hurricane Harvey, a category four storm, touched down on the Texas middle coast in August 2017. After four days of intense rain, some areas were deluged by more than 40 inches of water. The damage caused by the destructive and deadly storm shook America to its core.

On the Monday after the storm, a Dallas newspaper reported that some people held Sunday services at an outdoor athletics' track in south Texas where Hurricane Harvey had hit the hardest. Those who attended said it was important for them to be at church, despite the ravages of the storm. They were demonstrating their faith in Christ.

In his letter to the Roman church, Paul said that none of life's events can separate us from God's love. We are more than conquerors! The people in south Texas proved that devastating circumstances and calamities like Hurricane Harvey cannot prevent us from worshipping the true and living God. We will bless the Lord at all times. With our faith rooted and grounded in Christ, we are unshakable!

Prayer: *Living God, help us always to be steadfast, immovable and abounding in your work and love at all times. In Jesus' name and for his sake. Amen*

Thought for the day: I will trust in the Lord at all times.

D. L. Ellis-Johnson (Texas, US)

Count them one by one

Read Philippians 4:4–9

I will give thanks to the Lord with my whole heart; I will tell of all your wonderful deeds.
Psalm 9:1 (NRSV)

Once again I couldn't sleep. Unresolved fear and anxiety became magnified by the dark quiet. Praying only made me focus on my troubles even more and question if God really cared.

I snuggled under the covers, shut my eyes and began remembering the good things that had happened that day. As I counted them, the bright spots added up: an email, a phone call, a friend having a good day. Peace slowly replaced fear. Still awake, I listed things I had accomplished that day, no matter how trivial: washing up, doing the laundry. Contentment replaced restlessness.

Finally, I recited comforting Bible passages and prayers. By the end of this process, I was falling asleep, secure again that God really does care and is working in my life.

These three steps don't always cure insomnia, but with practice they help. When my brain thinks it's morning at 2.00 am, I eat a banana, drink some water and start the three steps over again. It's amazing how much more positive I have become each evening. And the habit of listing the good things in my life sets a mood of praise that is truly relaxing.

Prayer: *Dear God, may your love drive out our worries and give us peaceful sleep. Amen*

Thought for the day: God's love drives out my fears.

Genie Stoker (Arizona, US)

Investing in others

Read Matthew 5:13–16
Let your light shine before others, that they may see your good deeds and glorify your Father in heaven.
Matthew 5:16 (NIV)

In my earliest ministry with the young people at a small church, I had to start from scratch with no resources. Although I had no idea what I was doing, I also knew that God could use the youngsters at this church. I believed I could connect with them and be their pastor.

One day, God opened my opportunities when I was invited to join a group of neighbourhood boys who were playing football. Reluctantly, I decided to play – but only because I knew that I needed to take part in their lives if they were ever going to consider anything I would say or do. Early on, the ball rolled right to me. I kicked it and started running. After colliding with one of the boys, I managed to score a goal. Almost immediately, all these boys became a part of the youth ministry at the church.

My experiences in youth ministry taught me that if I want people to be interested in what I say, I first need to be interested in what they say and do. I have applied this principle right through my ministry: the good news of Jesus spreads first by embracing the lives of others. This is what I believe the incarnation of Jesus is truly all about.

Prayer: *Dear Lord Jesus, help us to reach into the lives of the people we meet every day to reflect to others the light of the love of God. Amen*

Thought for the day: I can spread the good news of Christ by taking an interest in the lives of others.

Cletus L. Hull III (Pennsylvania, US)

New life

Read Isaiah 43:16–21

I have come that they may have life, and have it to the full.
John 10:10 (NIV)

By late winter most of us have had enough of seeing bare, lifeless branches. Judging by the bigger picture, the colour, warmth and vibrance of spring seem far off. But if we go out into the garden and look at the smaller picture, we can see the beginnings of tiny shoots and the earliest signs of new life. Something is happening after all.

Sometimes our lives are a bit like that. We feel much the same and look the same from a distance, but up close God is at work in us – creating small changes. Little by little, God clothes us in more gifts and more love. We may summon up the courage to try something new. Often when we take that risk, we are surprised by the gifts that God has placed within us. We find that we are better at doing something than we thought we might be.

As we accept and enjoy these small changes, we sense God's love flourishing within us. Just as the first signs of spring are beginning to show in the garden, so God's spiritual gifts are taking root deep within us.

Prayer: *Living Lord, thank you for the new growth within us. Help us to trust your presence within us as we risk doing new things for you. Amen*

Thought for the day: God can make me new every morning.

Meg Mangan (New South Wales, Australia)

Unexpected lesson

Read Matthew 6:9–13

Your will be done.
Matthew 6:10 (NRSV)

Visiting Ruth in hospital, I realised I had seen her many times at church but did not really know her. 'My brain has been scanned so many times,' she told me. I asked what she would like me to pray for. I was expecting to hear requests such as healing, relief from pain or to go home soon. I was surprised when Ruth replied simply, 'Whatever is God's will and purpose for my being here, pray that it be fulfilled.'

She was living in pain and would rather have been enjoying time with her grandchildren and great-grandchildren, but in her prayer she put God's will first. She loved and trusted the Lord with all her heart.

A few weeks after my first visit, Ruth died. I wish I had known her longer. In our short time together she had a great influence on me, especially on my prayer life. I think of her often as I pray for others and myself. Praying for God's will and purpose to be fulfilled is fitting for all circumstances.

Prayer: *Sovereign God, help us always to put your will above our own desires as we pray, 'Our Father in heaven, hallowed be your name, your kingdom come, your will be done, on earth as it is in heaven. Give us today our daily bread. And forgive us our debts, as we also have forgiven our debtors. And lead us not into temptation, but deliver us from the evil one'* Amen*

Thought for the day: In all circumstances, I strive to be able to tell God, 'Your will be done.'

Bob Peterson (Texas, US)

Producing beauty

Read Galatians 5:16–25

*The fruit of the Spirit is love, joy, peace, forbearance, kindness,
goodness, faithfulness, gentleness and self-control.*
Galatians 5:22–23 (NIV)

On a recent trip to the garden centre, I was hoping to select a flowering
plant that would continue to produce beautiful blossoms throughout
the summer. The assistant told me to be sure to take off the faded flowers. That way the plant's energy would go into producing new flowers.

I began to think about my own life. Do I spend my time and energy
projecting God's beauty in the world or is my energy being wasted on
things that aren't life-giving? Do I harbour feelings of anger, jealousy or
resentment towards anyone? Do I waste my energy feeding my fears
and doubts? When I began to take an inventory of my thoughts and
feelings and how I spend my time, I came to realise that my negative
thoughts are using energy that could be used to allow God's light to
shine through me.

I followed the advice, and my plant produced beautiful flowers
throughout the summer. Each time I picked off the faded blooms,
I prayed for the wisdom and guidance to use my energy to produce
beauty in the world through kindness, joy and love.

Prayer: *Dear Lord, help us to learn from all your creation how to spread
the gospel message of peace, joy and love. Amen*

Thought for the day: What everyday tasks can teach me the ways of
God?

Andrea Woronick (Connecticut, US)

Invitation to witness

Read Mark 16:9–20

[Jesus] said to them, 'Go into all the world and proclaim the good news to the whole creation.'
Mark 16:15 (NRSV)

When I joined our church prayer fellowship, I shared the testimony of how I have been led closer to God. Then God cultivated within me a longing to share my faith in writing. At the time, however, I did not know where to start.

One day my husband came home with a devotional booklet called *Saat Teduh*, the Indonesian edition of *The Upper Room* daily devotional guide. As I began to read it, I immediately felt blessed by the testimonies of God's children from around the world. Though the reflections are brief, they are full of meaning, offering uplifting insights. *Saat Teduh* has become a companion to my Bible reading.

At the end of that issue, I noticed an invitation for readers to write their own reflections for possible publication. My thoughts quickly turned to thanksgiving because God had answered my longing to share my faith. Straight away, I wrote some reflections and sent them to the editor. But even if my work is not published, I know that God loves to see us eager to share our faith for the uplifting of his people.

Prayer: *Lord Jesus, help us to be your witnesses to the ends of the earth. Amen*

Thought for the day: What gifts do I have to witness for Christ?

Emiriana Malelak-Bana (East Nusa Tenggara, Indonesia)

Surrendering all

Read Luke 18:18–23

[Jesus] said to him, 'You still lack one thing. Sell everything you have and give to the poor, and you will have treasure in heaven. Then come, follow me.'

Luke 18:22 (NIV)

In 2017, I pleaded guilty to bank fraud. Due to my conviction, I was required to surrender my licence to practise as an accountant, which meant that I had to return my certificate. As I began removing the certificate from its frame, I started to cry when I saw the label that read 'Main Street Framing'. My parents had been so proud of my achievement that they had my certificate framed in my home town.

This experience made me think of the wealthy ruler in Luke 18. Up until this point, I had gone to church and lived a pretty straight-and-narrow life, but I had always put my career, success and money before God.

If we are intent on living an abundant and successful life, we will place a greater value on God and our relationship with him than on our worldly success, career, material possessions or anything else that stands between us and him. When we put God first and seek to follow his will in all that we do, we will have everything that we need. Only then can we experience true success.

Prayer: *Dear God, shape our hearts and desires so that we can follow your will for our lives. Amen*

Thought for the day: What am I putting ahead of my relationship with God?

Steve Wakefield (Georgia, US)

A different talent

Read 1 Corinthians 12:5–6, 12–27

There are different kinds of service, but the same Lord.
1 Corinthians 12:5 (NIV)

On holiday in Vienna, Austria, my husband and I took time to watch the famous Lipizzaner stallions. These beautiful horses performed elegant manoeuvres, precise and controlled steps, and amazing leaps. I was enthralled by their magnificence.

Later as we strolled through the old town of Vienna, I saw pairs of horses pulling carriages, giving tourists a relaxed view of the city. Their hooves clip-clopped on the path as they plodded along – no fancy manoeuvres or leaps for them. However, while these horses lacked the majesty of the Lipizzaner stallions, they still served a valuable purpose.

Sometimes I wish I could be like the Lipizzaners, elegant and applauded for my accomplishments. But maybe God wants me to humbly pull a carriage, serving others without reward or recognition. I think of the neighbours who gave us a lift to the airport, the other neighbour caring for our cat while we were away, the people at church who encourage us and make us feel welcome. I am grateful for these ordinary people serving God in quiet ways. They may gain little attention, but they receive great honour in God's eyes.

Prayer: *Dear Lord, help us to use the talents you have given us without looking for reward or recognition. Amen*

Thought for the day: How can I use my talents to serve God today?

Susan Thogerson Maas (Oregon, US)

Cycle of love

Read Matthew 22:36–40

Love your neighbour as yourself.
Matthew 22:39 (NIV)

Being a perfectionist, I can be pretty hard on myself when things don't go just right. Judgemental, condemning and merciless thoughts about myself often plague me: 'Why can't I be the loving person I want to be all the time? Three out of five times just won't do!' On one particular day when I had snapped for the third time in a row at an unsuspecting loved one, the condemning thoughts were about to flow. Then a new thought interrupted: 'You can't give what you don't have.' It was as if God were telling me that if I could love myself the way he loves me, I would be able to love others more fully.

It had never occurred to me how much loving others depended on loving myself. And it had never occurred to me how much I didn't love myself. It was a time of intense soul-searching. 'Does God condemn me? Is God merciless and unforgiving towards me? No.' I decided to suspend all thoughts about myself that didn't match God's thoughts of me. For the first time in a long time, I had genuine love for myself: forgiveness, grace, hope, peace, joy – and enough to share.

Although I continue to mess up at times, now only thoughts of forgiveness flow. I choose to keep on loving myself so that I will have an ample supply of God's love to give to others.

Prayer: *Merciful God, help us to see ourselves and others the way you do – as worth the love with which you love us. Amen*

Thought for the day: When I accept God's love for me, I can pour out that love on others.

Amorelle Browne (Grenada)

Finish the race

Read Philippians 3:10–14

I have fought the good fight, I have finished the race, I have kept the faith.
2 Timothy 4:7 (NIV)

I remember the day I watched my daughter's first marathon. While the gruelling physical toll is evident in the bodies of the athletes, the mental and emotional strain is not so clear – at least to the spectators. After five or six miles, the runners are hitting their stride. At mile 13, they sigh in relief and hope, but at around 20 miles, runners often 'hit the wall' and experience overwhelming exhaustion, wondering if they can continue. But still this challenge is not insurmountable for those with determination, adequate training and the desire to finish one of the toughest races anyone can pursue.

Witnessing that marathon taught me something about living the Christian life. Purpose, diligence and the willingness to place ourselves in the hands of God to see us through the most difficult tasks will help us to finish the race laid out before us.

Prayer: *Dear God, give us your strength in moments of weakness so that we can complete our life's race. In the name of your Son. Amen*

Thought for the day: If we persevere in faith, God will carry us to the end of our life's race.

David Payne (Missouri, US)

Taking the leap

Read Ecclesiastes 3:1–11

[God] has made everything beautiful in its time. He has also set eternity in the human heart.
Ecclesiastes 3:11 (NIV)

In the front garden, our bird box was home to a family of bluebirds. I was riveted to my binoculars as I watched the babies peer out one by one – some even hopping daringly on to the wooden edge of the box's opening. Probably sometime later that day they would discover that they could fly.

Is this the way God views my fledgling attempts to try new things? Does he get excited when I step out a little in faith and spread my wings? I recently flew from North Carolina to Austria for a prayer conference. It was exciting and scary to travel that far across the world by myself. But taking that somewhat frightening leap greatly deepened my faith and my prayer life.

God's mysterious gift of instinct moves in baby birds, leading them to stretch their wings and fly at exactly the right time. I pray to be given a similar inner direction when God wants me to try new areas of ministry or personal growth. May I always be willing to spread my wings and jump when God says it's time.

Prayer: *Dear God, give us the courage to try new things as you lead us into deeper paths on our journey of faith. Amen*

Thought for the day: I will be ready to take a leap of faith when God asks me.

Cynthia Harris (North Carolina, US)

Jesus around us

Read Matthew 25:31–46

Since there will never cease to be some in need on the earth,
I therefore command you, 'Open your hand to the poor and needy
neighbour in your land.'
Deuteronomy 15:11 (NRSV)

Jesus' words in Matthew 25 remind me of the importance of caring for the needs of those around me. This passage helps me to remember that Christ lives around us, and although we cannot see him face to face, we can see him in the faces of others. And we can reflect Christ's love through our actions. Every day, we have the opportunity to reach out to those in need and show them God's love. Christ wants us to be God's hands to touch them, God's heart to love them and God's ears to listen to their cries.

What a privilege it is to be able to give food to those who are hungry, to visit those who are ill or imprisoned or to pray with and encourage those who feel discouraged! We can be answers to the prayers of those in need. God trusts that we will attend to the cries of others. The excess that we have is someone's portion, placed in our hands by God. Let us give it willingly.

Prayer: *Dear Lord, help us see the ways we can care for the needs of others. Open our eyes to see Christ around us every day. Amen*

Thought for the day: When I give generously to others, I show them God's love.

Muyiwa Benralph Olaiya (Federal Capital Territory, Nigeria)

Deliverance

Read Psalm 3

From the Lord comes deliverance.

Psalm 3:8 (NIV)

Five years ago, my firstborn son was diagnosed with type 1 diabetes. This life-threatening disease requires checking his blood sugar and dosing him with insulin several times a day. At the same time, my own body has begun to betray me. With a recent hysterectomy, an inoperable labral tear and recurring migraines, I'm always struggling to keep my spirits up. These trials have made simple things, like getting a full night's sleep, much more difficult.

In the middle of the night, after a crisis with my son's glucose level, I tossed and turned for an hour trying to get back to sleep. Finally, I slowly got out of bed. With my Bible in hand, I intended to read Leviticus but instead opened to an old bookmark that said: 'Lord, how many are my foes! How many rise up against me!' (Psalm 3:1). The writer of this psalm was not so different from me. Though not the same as mine, his problems were as numerous. In the midst of them he turned to God: 'I call out to the Lord' (v. 4). And he trusted God to help him: 'From the Lord comes deliverance' (v. 8). Through this passage, God showed me that I am not alone, and that he can rescue me. No matter what our trials, God is faithful and will be present with us.

Prayer: *Dear Lord, thank you for caring for us through all our trials. Amen*

Thought for the day: The Lord is strong enough to deliver me.

Heidi Kupitz (Oregon, US)

God's handiwork

Read Romans 8:18–28

O Lord, you are our Father; we are the clay, and you are our potter; we are all the work of your hand.
Isaiah 64:8 (NRSV)

During a trip to celebrate our 40th wedding anniversary, my wife and I had the opportunity to see a glassblower at work. It was fascinating to watch. He blew through the long tube to produce a bubble of molten glass and continued to grow and shape it through heat and pressure. He then added what appeared to be coloured dust and eventually produced a beautiful bowl that we now have on our mantelpiece.

This reminded me of the prophet Isaiah's words in which a similar process makes us beautiful and useful for God. While the glassblower added the 'coloured dust' to give the bowl its beauty, it was the heat and pressure together that formed its final shape and substance. I do not always understand or like the 'pressures' or 'heat' of life's tough times. But I believe that God uses them to make me the person he intends me to be. I believe in the love and goodness of God. When we place our lives in his hands each day, we can trust that he is at work in us for our ultimate spiritual good and for God's ultimate glory.

Prayer: *O God, help us to see every situation as an opportunity to become more like the image of your Son, Jesus. Amen*

Thought for the day: The pressures of life allow God to shape me.

J. Leland Collins Jr. (Virginia, US)

Small group questions

Wednesday 6 May

1 Have you ever been given a challenge to express your faith like today's writer was? If so, how did your experience change the way you think about your faith? If not, would you ever consider participating in something like this?

2 How do you express your faith? How do those expressions of faith enrich your life and the lives of those around you?

3 Have you ever felt as if you were unable to follow God because you didn't have the time or the money? When you are distracted by the busyness of life, who or what helps you to regain your focus on serving God?

4 What outreach programmes does your church offer, and how do you participate? What new ministries do you think your church should start?

5 Do you try to maintain your Lenten disciplines all year, or is it good to have certain practices for certain seasons? Why?

Wednesday 13 May

1 Describe a time when you have witnessed the power of prayer. How did that experience affect your faith? If the situation had been resolved differently, would your faith have been affected in a different way? Why or why not?

2 What scripture passages remind you of the importance of prayer? How do those verses encourage you as you pray?

3 Do you always trust in God when you pray? Do you ever pray without fully trusting? What helps strengthen your trust in God?

4 Describe a time when you prayed and received a seemingly impossible result or a time when you prayed and did not receive the answer you were hoping for. How did you feel? How did you maintain your faith during this time?

5   In what ways can you support someone who has received an unwanted outcome to prayer? What encouragement can you offer to someone who is currently struggling to pray?

Wednesday 20 May

1   Have you ever thought, like today's writer, that mission statements are only for companies and businesses? What do you think of the idea that you can write a personal mission statement? What would your mission statement be?

2   Do you ever struggle with staying focused spiritually? If not, how do you avoid distractions? If so, do you think a mission statement would help you? What other practices might be beneficial?

3   What spiritual practices help you to listen to God? If you already know what assignment God has given you, how did you discern it? How does having an assignment change the way you live out your faith?

4   Name some biblical characters who had a clear mission and remained focused. Which biblical characters did not remain true to their mission?

5   How does your church encourage you to find your spiritual mission? In what ways can you encourage others to do the same?

Wednesday 27 May

1   When have you had a change of heart? Describe the situation and how it affected you. Did you share your change of heart with others? How did they respond?

2   Share your thoughts about multiracial churches or communities. In what ways can you work to be more open to leaders and community members who are different from you?

3   Today's writer is encouraged by remembering that we fulfil God's ministry when we meet others 'heart to heart in Christ's love'. What does this mean to you? In what ways can you be more intentional about connecting with others?

4 When have you been in a situation in which you felt unable to minister to others? What obstacles prevented you from ministering to them? What prayers, scripture passages, spiritual practices or people helped you find strength in the situation?

5 Where do you see cultural differences in your church, community and the world? Name some examples of stories or people who have embraced differences and strengthened their community by doing so. What hope or inspiration do you draw from these examples?

Wednesday 3 June

1 Describe a time when you learned more from someone's actions than you did from their words. How can you apply what you learned in that situation to other relationships?

2 The writer of today's meditation appears to have accepted her husband's musical preference willingly. What if you try to reach out to someone and they reject your efforts? How could you remain encouraged in such a situation?

3 Do you think it is more important to minister to others through words or through actions? Why?

4 Which biblical characters demonstrated their faith through their words and actions? How does their example encourage you? In what ways can you follow their example?

5 What does it mean to you to live your faith? Who serves as an example of faith to you? How can you show them how much their example means to you?

Wednesday 10 June

1 Have you ever become reconciled with someone with whom you had a difficult relationship? If so, describe how that reconciliation affected you and changed the relationship.

2 The writer's brother reached out to the writer multiple times trying to make amends. What do you do when you apologise to someone, but they don't respond in the way you had hoped? What do you do when someone apologises to you, but you don't want to forgive them?

3 Have you ever thought about forgiveness as a chance to see the face of God? If so, what does that mean to you? If not, does that idea change the way you think about forgiveness?

4 What spiritual practices and prayers help you to let go of bitterness? What biblical passages remind you of the importance of forgiveness? In what ways do these help you?

5 How does your church help members who have disagreements? In what ways could your church better help its members to be reconciled after a conflict? How can you encourage those changes in your church?

Wednesday 17 June

1 Have you ever prayed that someone would change their personality? Do you think this is a good thing to pray for? Discuss why or why not.

2 Describe a time when you realised that you had been praying for the wrong thing. How did you realise it? In what ways did you change your prayers? What was the outcome?

3 The writer's friends helped her decide to change her prayers. How have your friends helped you grow in your faith? Which biblical friends serve as mentors for you in your own friendships? Why?

4 How do you remind yourself to be accepting and understanding of your differences with others? What encouragement can you offer to those who are challenged in accepting someone's differences?

5 When have you experienced the Holy Spirit guiding your prayers? How did that change your perspective? How do you know when your prayers are getting off track? What do you do to refocus your prayers?

Wednesday 24 June

1 Describe a time when you felt unsure of your ability to fulfil a need. How did you respond, and what was the outcome of the situation? What did this experience teach you about yourself and your abilities?

2 Before volunteering at her church, today's writer identified with Moses. With which biblical character do you most identify at the moment? Why? What can you learn from that character?

3 When you see a need, are you eager to step in and fulfil it? Or, like today's writer, do you stay quiet and hope that others will volunteer? Would you like to change the way you respond? If so, what practical steps can you take to do so?

4 When you feel God nudging you out of your comfort zone, how do you react? What prayers bring you peace when you are apprehensive about taking a new path? How do those around you encourage you to do things that intimidate you?

5 What needs do you currently see in your church? In your community? In the world? What can you do to help meet those needs? What can you encourage those around you to do?

Wednesday 1 July

1 Describe the handwriting of a loved one. What do you think this person's handwriting says about their personality?

2 What reflections of God do you see around you? How can you learn more about God by studying the strokes of his hands? How will you make time to study God's handiwork today?

3 Today's writer describes ways we can come to know God more. What other ways can you think of to grow closer to him? In what ways can these practices help you?

4 How do your relationships with others help you to see God's handiwork? How do your interactions with nature do this? Do you find that you need to look intentionally to see reflections of God, or do they appear when you least expect them?

5 What do you hope to reflect to others? What can you do intentionally to reflect these qualities? How would your community change if
everyone focused on reflecting God?

Wednesday 8 July

1 When have you chosen not to do something for someone and later
regretted your decision? What do you wish you had done differently?
How did you learn and grow from this experience?

2 Do you naturally feel pulled to defend and help others, or do you
often need to convince yourself to step in? Why do you think this is?
What helps you choose to help others when you might prefer to stay
out of the situation?

3 Name biblical characters who inspire you to reach out to those who
are being bullied or need help. What do you admire about them?
How do their examples affect your choices?

4 What small acts have you witnessed that have ultimately had a big
impact on a person? What can you do to make a difference like that
in someone's life?

5 In what ways do you reach out to and stand up for those in your community? How do your loved ones and your church encourage you in
your efforts? How can you support others as they also reach out and
stand up for those around them?

Wednesday 15 July

1 Have others ever made you feel that you need to change parts of your
personality? If so, what brought you comfort during that time? How
can you encourage someone who is experiencing similar pressures?

2 Do you think Christians should behave a certain way – calm and
quiet, loud and inquisitive, or somewhere in between? Or do you
think Christians should embrace their natural personality traits?
How would your church community change if every member either
embraced their natural personality or adopted a specific way
of behaving?

3 Do you know who you are in God? If so, how has that helped you reach out to others? If not, what do you think will help you discover who you are in him?

4 What scriptures remind you of the importance of accepting and loving others as they are? When you find it difficult to accept someone, what prayers help you overcome such feelings?

5. How does it encourage you to know that God loves you even when you don't love yourself? What helps you to remember that? How can you remind others that God loves them?

Wednesday 22 July

1 Describe a time when you realised your need for a disciplined approach to a task or situation. How did changing your method help you reach your goal? How can you apply what you learned from that experience to other situations?

2 What spiritual disciplines bring you closer to God? How do you remain committed when beginning a new spiritual practice? Do you think there is a time or place for spirituality without specific disciplines? Why or why not?

3 What changes do you see in your life and your relationship with God when you direct your heart towards him? What happens when you lose focus on God? How do you refocus on your relationship with him when you get distracted?

4 What does it look like when God comes near to you? How do you know when he is near? In what ways are you comforted by knowing that he is close?

5 What spiritual disciplines does your church prioritise? What spiritual disciplines would you like to see more of in your congregation? How can you participate more actively in the spiritual practices your church offers?

Wednesday 29 July

1 Today's writer remembers a special time with her family. What special times bring you closer to your family? Talk about a time spent with your family that is particularly memorable.

2 Name some people whom you tend to avoid or overlook based on outward appearances or first impressions. How have you found these first impressions to be inaccurate? What can you do to help others see that they are valued?

3 Have you ever been put off by something Jesus does in scripture? Why? What in the story challenges you most? What has the story taught you about how Jesus wants us to treat others?

4 Describe a time when you tasted God's goodness. Did that taste make you desire to follow Jesus? What does it look like for you to follow Jesus wherever he leads?

5 How can you share the goodness of God with others? What specific actions and services can you do for those in your community to give them a positive impression of Jesus?

Wednesday 5 August

1 If you have ever been part of a prayer chain, describe your experience. How did you see prayer working in your life and in the lives of others? How is praying as part of a group different from praying alone?

2 When have you felt distant from other Christians? What helped you reconnect with your Christian community?

3 What does it mean to you to 'pray scripture' like today's writer does? How do you prefer to pray? Describe how your prayer practice enriches your prayer life.

4 What sort of prayer outreach ministry does your church offer? How can you engage more fully with it? What new prayer ministry would you like your church to start?

5 Name some people in the Bible who remind you of the importance of prayer. What do you most admire about how these people prayed? How can you follow their examples?

Wednesday 12 August

1 Do you dislike waiting as much as today's writer does? When has waiting been especially difficult for you? What does it mean to be 'open as we wait'?

2 Describe a time when you had to adjust your attitude. What changes did you notice in yourself and your situation after the adjustment? How do you stay mindful of your attitude?

3 Does it ever feel that waiting on God is a waste of time? Why or why not? What scripture passages comfort you and remind you that God is always at work in your life? Why do these passages bring you comfort?

4 What does it look like for God to renew your strength? How do other Christians help to restore your strength? How can you help strengthen others when they are struggling?

5 In what ways can waiting patiently change your life? How can it change your church? How might it change the world? Name ways you can embrace waiting and encourage others to do so.

Wednesday 19 August

1 Describe a time when you were invited to participate in something you didn't want to do. How did you respond? In what ways did your choice affect your relationships with others?

2 How do you feel towards someone when they take an interest in what interests you? How do you feel when someone shows no interest in what interests you? What do your reactions in these situations teach you about how you want to treat others?

3   What does it mean to invest in the lives of others? What spiritual practices help you make space for others in your heart and mind? How does investing in others enable you to share the love of Christ with them?

4   Name a story in the Bible that shows you what it means to embrace the lives of others. How can you apply that example to your life and the way you invest in others?

5   Who in your life serves as an example of investing in others? In what ways does this person enrich your life? How can you tell them how much you admire them and their example?

Wednesday 26 August

1   When your mind is filled with condemning thoughts, how do you change your perspective? What practices, prayers or people help you remember to fill your mind with loving thoughts?

2   Have you ever felt unable to love others in the way you would like? What do you think prevents you from loving others? What might help you to love others when you are struggling to do so?

3   In what ways does it comfort you to know that God loves you unconditionally? How does staying mindful of his love change the way you love yourself and others?

4   How can you encourage someone and show them God's unconditional love? What prayers, scripture passages, words of encouragement or companionship can you offer someone who needs God's love?

5   Name some Bible verses that remind you of the importance of love, forgiveness, grace, hope, peace and joy. How can you incorporate these verses into your spiritual life? What practices can help you remember God's love for you?

Journal page

Journal page

Journal page

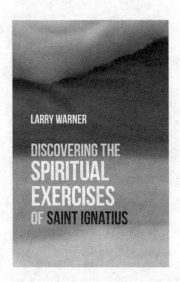

This book is an adaptation of the Spiritual Exercises of St Ignatius Loyola, to help you to embark on a life-transforming journey towards Christlikeness. This is not a book about the methods or techniques of Christian formation but one that enables you to come before God through the gospel narratives in order to encounter Jesus afresh. If you hunger for something deeper, yearn to walk with Jesus (not just read about him) and desire to embrace more of what God is doing in and through you, then this is the book for you.

Discovering the Spiritual Exercises of Saint Ignatius
Larry Warner
978 0 85746 977 9 £12.99
brfonline.org.uk

Using the biblical idea of pilgrimage, Sally Welch walks alongside us as leader and guide, but also fellow traveller, to explore how we can understand this principle and make it our own. The book is divided into sections of a journey, beginning with the preparations necessary before setting out, exploring the obstacles that might be put in our path and sharing ways in which the journey can be made easier and more productive. At the end of each reflection Sally suggests an activity or prayer to enable the reader to apply the learning to their own life.

Journey to Contentment
Pilgrimage principles for everyday life
Sally Welch
978 0 85746 592 4 £8.99
brfonline.org.uk

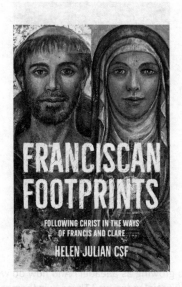

There are many ways of following Christ – each footprint is unique. One of these, the Franciscan spiritual journey, has been tried and tested over the centuries, and the experiences of Francis and Clare and all those who have been inspired by their lives still resonate with us. Helen Julian CSF explores the distinctive features of their spirituality and shows how these practices can be applied to, and become part of, our daily lives. Through stories of care for creation, social justice, mission, preaching, contemplative spirituality and simple living, discover your own pathway today.

Franciscan Footprints
Following Christ in the ways of Francis and Clare
Helen Julian CSF
978 0 85746 811 6 £8.99
brfonline.org.uk

How do we keep growing as a leader? And how do we ensure others around us grow in their leadership? These twin themes run throughout this book, exploring the joys and challenges of leading at a time when we need Christians to lead well wherever they are. Such leadership is always about more than just skills. It includes a clearer sense of call, growth in Christlike character, an ability to lead well with others and, at heart, a deepening relationship with God. This books offer practical ideas and insights into how to grow as this sort of leader.

Growing Leaders – fully revised and updated
Reflections on leadership, life and Jesus
James Lawrence
978 0 85746 888 8 £10.99
brfonline.org.uk

SHARING OUR VISION – MAKING A GIFT

I would like to make a gift to support BRF. Please use my gift for:

- [ ] BRF charity   [ ] Barnabas in Schools   [ ] Parenting for Faith
- [ ] Messy Church   [ ] Anna Chaplaincy   [ ] where it is most needed

Title	First name/initials	Surname

Address	
	Postcode

Email

Telephone

Signature	Date

giftaid it   You can add an extra 25p to every £1 you give.

Please treat as Gift Aid donations all qualifying gifts of money made

[ ] today,   [ ] in the past four years,   [ ] and in the future.

I am a UK taxpayer and understand that if I pay less Income Tax and/or Capital Gains Tax in the current tax year than the amount of Gift Aid claimed on all my donations, it is my responsibility to pay any difference.

[ ] My donation does not qualify for Gift Aid.

Please notify BRF if you want to cancel this Gift Aid declaration, change your name or home address, or no longer pay sufficient tax on your income and/or capital gains.

Please complete other side of form ➲

Please return this form to:
BRF, 15 The Chambers, Vineyard, Abingdon OX14 3FE

The Bible Reading Fellowship is a Registered Charity (233280)

SHARING OUR VISION – MAKING A GIFT

Regular giving

By Direct Debit: You can set up a Direct Debit quickly and easily at **brf.org.uk/donate**

By Standing Order: Please contact our Fundraising Administrator +44 (0)1865 319700 | **giving@brf.org.uk**

One-off donation

Please accept my gift of:

☐ £10 ☐ £50 ☐ £100 Other £ [   ]

by (*delete as appropriate*):

☐ Cheque/Charity Voucher payable to 'BRF'

☐ MasterCard/Visa/Debit card/Charity card

Name on card [   ]

Card no. [ ][ ][ ][ ] [ ][ ][ ][ ] [ ][ ][ ][ ] [ ][ ][ ][ ]

Expires end [M M][Y Y] Security code* [   ]

*Last 3 digits on the reverse of the card
ESSENTIAL IN ORDER TO PROCESS
YOUR PAYMENT

Signature [   ] Date [   ]

☐ I would like to leave a gift in my will to BRF.

For more information, visit **brf.org.uk/lastingdifference**

For help or advice regarding making a gift, please contact our Fundraising Administrator +44 (0)1865 319700

(FR) Registered with
FUNDRAISING
REGULATOR

⮌ Please complete other side of form

Please return this form to:
BRF, 15 The Chambers, Vineyard, Abingdon OX14 3FE

The Bible Reading Fellowship is a Registered Charity (233280)

UR0220

How to encourage Bible reading in your church

BRF has been helping individuals connect with the Bible for over 90 years. We want to support churches as they seek to encourage church members into regular Bible reading.

Order a Bible reading resources pack

This pack is designed to give your church the tools to publicise our Bible reading notes. It includes:

- Sample Bible reading notes for your congregation to try.
- Publicity resources, including a poster.
- A church magazine feature about Bible reading notes.

The pack is free, but we welcome a £5 donation to cover the cost of postage. If you require a pack to be sent outside the UK or require a specific number of sample Bible reading notes, please contact us for postage costs. More information about what the current pack contains is available on our website.

How to order and find out more

- Visit **biblereadingnotes.org.uk/for-churches**.
- Telephone BRF on +44 (0)1865 319700 Mon–Fri 9.15–17.30.
- Write to us at BRF, 15 The Chambers, Vineyard, Abingdon OX14 3FE.

Keep informed about our latest initiatives

We are continuing to develop resources to help churches encourage people into regular Bible reading, wherever they are on their journey. Join our email list at **brfonline.org.uk/signup** to stay informed about the latest initiatives that your church could benefit from.

Subscriptions

The Upper Room is published in January, May and September.

Individual subscriptions
The subscription rate for orders for 4 or fewer copies includes postage and packing:

The Upper Room annual individual subscription   £17.85

Group subscriptions
Orders for 5 copies or more, sent to ONE address, are post free:
The Upper Room annual group subscription   £14.10

Please do not send payment with order for a group subscription. We will send an invoice with your first order.

Please note that the annual billing period for group subscriptions runs from 1 May to 30 April.

Copies of the notes may also be obtained from Christian bookshops.

Single copies of *The Upper Room* cost £4.70.

Prices valid until 30 April 2021.

Giant print version
The Upper Room is available in giant print for the visually impaired, from:

Torch Trust for the Blind
Torch House
Torch Way
Northampton Road
Market Harborough
LE16 9HL

Tel: +44 (0)1858 438260
torchtrust.org

THE UPPER ROOM: INDIVIDUAL/GIFT SUBSCRIPTION FORM

All our Bible reading notes can be ordered online by visiting
brfonline.org.uk/collections/subscriptions

❑ I would like to take out a subscription myself (complete your name and
address details once)

❑ I would like to give a gift subscription (please provide both names and
addresses)

Title .... First name/initials .... Surname ....

Address ....

.... Postcode ....

Telephone .... Email ....

Gift subscription name ....

Gift subscription address ....

.... Postcode ....

Gift message (20 words max. or include your own gift card):

....

....

Please send *The Upper Room* beginning with the September 2020 /
January 2021 / May 2021 issue (*delete as appropriate*):

Annual individual subscription ❑ £17.85   Total enclosed £ ....

Method of payment

❑ Cheque (made payable to BRF) ❑ MasterCard / Visa

Card no. ☐☐☐☐ ☐☐☐☐ ☐☐☐☐ ☐☐☐☐

Expires end ☐☐ ☐☐   Security code* ☐☐☐   Last 3 digits on the
reverse of the card

*ESSENTIAL IN ORDER TO PROCESS THE PAYMENT

All our Bible reading notes can be ordered online by visiting brfonline.org.uk/collections/subscriptions

❏ Please send me .... copies of *The Upper Room* September 2020 / January 2021 / May 2021 issue (*delete as appropriate*)

Title .... First name/initials .... Surname ....

Address ....

.... Postcode ....

Telephone .... Email ....

Please do not send payment with this order. We will send an invoice with your first order.

Christian bookshops: All good Christian bookshops stock BRF publications. For your nearest stockist, please contact BRF.

Telephone: The BRF office is open Mon–Fri 9.15–17.30. To place your order, telephone +44 (0)1865 319700.

Online: brfonline.org.uk/pages/group-subscriptions

❏ Please send me a Bible reading resources pack to encourage Bible reading in my church

Please return this form with the appropriate payment to:
BRF, 15 The Chambers, Vineyard, Abingdon OX14 3FE
To read our terms and find out about cancelling your order, please visit **brfonline.org.uk/terms**.

The Bible Reading Fellowship is a Registered Charity (233280)

To order

Online: brfonline.org.uk
Telephone: +44 (0)1865 319700 Mon–Fri 9.15–17.30

Delivery times within the UK are normally 15 working days. Prices are correct at the time of going to press but may change without prior notice.

Title	Price	Qty	Total
Discovering the Spiritual Exercises of St Ignatius	£12.99		
Journey to Contentment	£8.99		
Franciscan Footprints	£8.99		
Growing Leaders	£10.99		

POSTAGE AND PACKING CHARGES			
Order value	UK	Europe	Rest of world
Under £7.00	£2.00		
£7.00–£29.99	£3.00	Available on request	Available on request
£30.00 and over	FREE		

Total value of books	
Postage and packing	
Donation	
Total for this order	

Please complete in BLOCK CAPITALS

Title .... First name/initials .... Surname...

Address...

.... Postcode ....

Acc. No. .... Telephone ....

Email ....

Method of payment

❏ Cheque (made payable to BRF) ❏ MasterCard / Visa

Card no. ☐☐☐☐ ☐☐☐☐ ☐☐☐☐ ☐☐☐☐

Expires end ☐M☐M ☐Y☐Y Security code* ☐☐☐ Last 3 digits on the reverse of the card

Signature* .... Date .... /............ /............

*ESSENTIAL IN ORDER TO PROCESS THE PAYMENT

The Bible Reading Fellowship Gift Aid Declaration *giftaid it*

Please treat as Gift Aid donations all qualifying gifts of money made

❏ today, ❏ in the past four years, ❏ and in the future **or** ❏ My donation does not qualify for Gift Aid.

I am a UK taxpayer and understand that if I pay less Income Tax and/or Capital Gains Tax in the current tax year than the amount of Gift Aid claimed on all my donations, it is my responsibility to pay any difference.

Please notify BRF if you want to cancel this declaration, change your name or home address, or no longer pay sufficient tax on your income and/or capital gains.

Please return this form to: BRF, 15 The Chambers, Vineyard, Abingdon OX14 3FE | **enquiries@brf.org.uk**
To read our terms and find out about cancelling your order, please visit **brfonline.org.uk/terms**.

The Bible Reading Fellowship (BRF) is a Registered Charity (233280)